TOEIC®
VOCABULARY PREP

KAPLAN

PUBLISHING

ACKNOWLEDGMENTS

Special thanks to the team that made this book possible:

Kim Bowers, Lola Dart, Alexis Ferreri, Joanna Graham, Allison Harm, Richard J. Lapierre, Shmuel Ross, and many others who have contributed materials and advice over the years.

TOEIC® is a registered trademark of the Educational Testing Service, which neither sponsors nor endorses this product.

This publication is designed to provide accurate information in regard to the subject matter covered as of its publication date, with the understanding that knowledge and best practice constantly evolve. The publisher is not engaged in rendering medical, legal, accounting, or other professional service. If medical or legal advice or other expert assistance is required, the services of a competent professional should be sought. This publication is not intended for use in clinical practice or the delivery of medical care. To the fullest extent of the law, neither the Publisher nor the Editors assume any liability for any injury and/or damage to persons or property arising out of or related to any use of the material contained in this book.

Published by Kaplan Publishing, a division of Kaplan, Inc.
750 Third Avenue
New York, NY 10017

Printed in the United States of America

10 9 8 7 6 5 4 3 2 1

ISBN: 978-1-62523-339-4

Kaplan Publishing print books are available at special quantity discounts to use for sales promotions, employee premiums, or educational purposes. For more information or to purchase books, please call the Simon & Schuster special sales department at 866-506-1949.

TABLE OF CONTENTS

Section I: Vocabulary

Section 2: Idioms

K

Section 3: Exercises

Section 4: Answers

HOW TO USE THIS BOOK

The TOEIC® is a standardized test designed to measure your ability to understand and use English as it is used in a North American business setting. Recent changes to the TOEIC have shifted its focus from how much you know about English to how well you comprehend, speak, and write English.

This book is perfectly designed to help you learn more than 500 important TOEIC® vocabulary words. Simply read the vocabulary word and its part of speech on the front of a page to determine whether you know it. On the reverse side, its definition and a sample sentence are offered to be sure that you understand the word's meaning and its correct usage.

These sample sentences are followed by the corresponding noun, verb, adjective, or adverb forms. Thus you may learn four or more new words with each entry and increase your grasp of English grammar as well as your vocabulary.

You will notice that the words are not alphabetical or grouped by category. This is to help you focus on each individual word, its meaning, and its context. Words listed alphabetically are harder to distinguish and learn because they look and sound alike. Words grouped by category are easier to guess the meaning of without truly learning their meanings.

An idiom is a word or phrase that has a special meaning apart from its literal translation—it is usually a metaphor. Only people who are good at speaking English will know what an idiom means. Idioms can be difficult to learn, and they require time and patience to master well. With this book, you will learn more than 400 important idioms. Read the idiom on the front of the page to determine whether you know it; on the reverse side, its definition and a sample sentence are offered to be sure that you understand its correct usage.

You will also see some notes in square brackets [ ]. These provide additional information about the origins of the idiom that should make it easier to memorize. In some cases—mainly with verb phrases—some words are interchangeable. In such situations, two example sentences are provided, one for each version. The most common version appears first.

Study the words and idioms in any order and start on any page.

Good luck!

exclaim
exclaiming, exclaimed
verb

vacant
adjective

accept
accepting, accepted
verb

revolve
revolving, revolved
verb

pose
posing, posed
verb

proclaim, shout
*When he finally saw the company's profit sheet, he **exclaimed** with joy.*
n. exclamation, exclaimer

---

unused; empty
*The office next to his had been **vacant** for more than a year.*
n. vacancy, vacantness; adv. vacantly

---

1. to agree
2. to receive
*1. He chose to **accept** the company's proposal for the new building because it was the cheapest bid.*
*2. Please **accept** any packages that come for me while I am on vacation.*
adj. acceptable; n. acceptance

---

to rotate; to move in a circular motion
*The moon **revolves** around the earth.*
n. revolution

---

to present an attitude, position or stance
*After talking it over with my boss, I will **pose** an important question to the group.*
n. pose

excavate

excavating, excavated

verb

tentative

adjective

abandon

abandoning, abandoned

verb

trigger

triggering, triggered

verb

volunteer

volunteering, volunteered

verb

to make a hole by removing something
*They plan to **excavate** the ancient ruins to uncover more about the society.*
adj. excavated; n. excavation, excavator

---

unsure; undecided
*Because I don't know whether or not I will work on Sunday, I made **tentative** plans with my brother.*
adv. tentatively; n. tentativeness

---

to leave or forsake
*She is not allowed to **abandon** her post until the next officer arrives for duty.*
n. abandonment, abandoner; adj. abandoned

---

to cause (something) to happen; to set off
*The CEO's unexpected visit will likely **trigger** a bit of panic in the office.*
n. trigger

---

to offer to do something, usually without being asked, pressured, or paid
*John asked the group for someone to take the project, and Liz **volunteered**.*
n. volunteer; adj. voluntary; adv. voluntarily

predict
predicting, predicted
verb

---

accompany
accompanying, accompanied
verb

---

relax
relaxing, relaxed
verb

---

approve
approving, approved
verb

---

restrict
restricting, restricted
verb

to state what will happen in the future; to foresee
*It's difficult to **predict** whether the clients will renew their contract next year.*
n. prediction, predictability; adj. predictable; adv. predictably

to go or come along with
*The president's assistant **accompanied** him to Japan.*
n. accompaniment

to become less tense; to slacken
*A massage will help your muscles **relax**.*
n. relaxation; adj. relaxing, relaxed

1. to consent to, to allow, or to endorse
2. to believe to be correct or good
*1. The accounting department has to **approve** all expenses.*
*2. His parents don't **approve** of his career choice.*
n. approval; adj. approving; adv. approvingly

to limit; to reduce
*Overtime laws in California **restrict** how many hours a person can work in a day without being entitled to extra pay.*
n. restriction; adj. restrictive; adv. restrictively

violate
violating, violated
verb

deny
denying, denied
verb

immigrate
immigrating, immigrated
verb

conform
conforming, conformed
verb

acknowledge
acknowledging, acknowledged
verb

to defy; to disobey
*Speaking to the press will **violate** the contract.*
n. violation

---

1. to dispute the truth of (a statement or fact)
2. to reject or refuse (a request)
1. *Peter **denied** that he had used the company credit card.*
2. *They **denied** our request for an extension.*
n. denial; adj. deniable

---

to move to a new country
*Approximately one million people **immigrate** to the United States each year.*
n. immigration, immigrant

---

1. to follow rules or standards
2. to follow social conventions to fit in
1. *The presentation must **conform** to the guidelines of the client.*
2. *Unlike his free-spirited, artistic sister, he has always tried to **conform**.*
n. conformity, conformist; adj. conformist

---

to admit or accept as a fact; to recognize
*You should **acknowledge** that your mistakes caused us to miss the deadline.*
n. acknowledgment; adj. acknowledged

attract
attracting, attracted
verb

---

doctrine
noun

---

audible
adjective

---

unite
uniting, united
verb

---

train
training, trained
verb

to draw toward
*Because of the high pay, the role was able to **attract** many outstanding candidates.*
n. attraction; adj. attractable

---

theory; belief; principle
*The company's **doctrine** always puts the client first.*
adj. doctrinal

---

able to be heard
*The music was barely **audible** over the child crying in the lobby.*
adv. audibly; n. audibility, audibleness

---

to join or combine
*Despite the problems the two executives had experienced in the past, they were able to **unite** on the issue of human rights.*
adj. united; n. union, unity

---

to teach to do something, often by repetition
*It took almost three months to **train** her new assistant.*
adj. trained; n. training, trainer, trainee

memory
noun

---

fact
noun

---

cognizant
adjective

---

assemble
assembling, assembled
verb

---

expose
exposing, exposed
verb

1. the ability to recall information and experiences
2. something recollected from the past
1. *Because Sarah had a great **memory**, she was able to tell stories of her past experiences in vivid detail, even if they had happened years ago.*
2. *Mark was haunted by **memories** of losing the large client contract.*
v. memorize

---

something that is true
*Because Tony was very trustworthy, Jenny took everything he said as **fact**.*
adj. factual

---

to be aware of something
*She was **cognizant** that her directions could have been clearer.*

---

1. to put (something) together
2. to come together
1. *He will **assemble** the engine from spare parts.*
2. *All employees will **assemble** in the conference room at 3:00 p.m.*
n. assembly, assemblage

---

1. to reveal; to uncover
2. to make vulnerable; to put in contact with something dangerous
1. *The journalist wants to **expose** a bribery scandal in the mayor's office.*
2. *An explosion in the factory would **expose** workers to dangerous chemicals.*
n. exposure, exposé; adj. exposed

interpret
interpreting, interpreted
verb

---

demonstrate
demonstrating, demonstrated
verb

---

adjust
adjusting, adjusted
verb

---

diminish
diminishing, diminished
verb

---

acquire
acquiring, acquire
verb

to explain or understand the meaning of; to translate
*She says that she can **interpret** people's dreams.*
n. interpretation, interpreter; adj. interpretive

---

to show, to prove, or to establish (a principle, theory, etc.) with evidence
*The company said a study will **demonstrate** that their new medication is five times as effective as the medication offered by a competitor.*
n. demonstration, demonstrator; adj. demonstrable, demonstrative; adv. demonstrably, demonstratively

---

to change or alter (something) slightly in order to improve it; to modify
*You should **adjust** the font size of the report to a larger size*
n. adjustment adj. adjusted

---

to become less or worse; to decline
*His influence in the company is going to **diminish** after his successor is chosen.*
adj. diminished, diminishing

---

to obtain or receive; to attain
*During her year in Berlin, she expects to **acquire** a large German vocabulary.*
n. acquisition

influence
influencing, influenced
verb

revise
revising, revised
verb

absorb
absorbing, absorbed
verb

purchase
purchasing, purchased
verb

select
selecting, selected
verb

to have an effect on; to affect; to impact
*Current financial situations **influence** his decision.*
n. influence; adj. influential, influenced

---

to improve (a piece of writing, etc.) by changing it
*My boss suggested I **revise** the report again.*
n. revision, revisionism; adj. revised, revisionary, revisionist

---

to take in or soak up
*The paper towel could **absorb** only a small amount of the coffee he spilled.*
n. absorption; adj. absorbed, absorbing

---

to buy
*They are raising money to **purchase** new computers for the school.*
n. purchase, purchaser

---

to choose
*The clients will **select** their favorite campaign.*
n. selection, selector; adj. selective, select; adv. selectively

predecessor
noun

---

corporate
adjective

---

invent
inventing, invented
verb

---

create
creating, created
verb

---

commemorate
commemorating, commemorated
verb

something that comes before something else
*The company executives studied the successes of their **predecessors** so they could learn by example.*
v. precede

---

pertaining to a corporation or company
*Now that he was in the **corporate** world, he had to purchase a business-casual wardrobe.*

---

to produce something new
*Alexander Graham Bell **invented** the telephone.*
n. inventor, invention

---

to make something from scratch
*She was able to **create** beautiful works of art.*
adj. created; n. creator, creation

---

to honor something; to remember something
*Each year, he **commemorates** his national championship win by watching a recording of the game.*
n. commemorator, commemoration

mention
mentioning, mentioned
verb

---

formulate
formulating, formulated
verb

---

solve
solving, solved
verb

---

intervene
intervening, intervened
verb

---

enhance
enhancing, enhanced
verb

to bring something up; to refer to something
*She tried to **mention** the power of positive thinking whenever she could.*
adj. mentioned, mentionable

---

to come up; to develop
*Before Susan took any action, she decided to **formulate** a plan.*
n. formulation, formulator

---

to come up with an answer to a something
*After much thinking, he was able to **solve** the problem of inventory loss.*
adj. solved

---

to become involved in a situation; to interfere
*Before the confrontation escalated, she decided to **intervene** and change the subject.*
n. intervention; adj. intervening

---

to make better; to improve
*Dressing professionally for a job interview will **enhance** your chances of getting hired.*
n. enhancement; adj. enhanced

motivate
motivating, motivated
verb

imply
implying, implied
verb

reveal
revealing, revealed
verb

implement
implementing, implemented
verb

thrive
thriving, thrived/throve
verb

to give (a person) a reason or incentive to do something; to encourage or inspire
*Our manager tries to **motivate** us to work harder by having us set goals.*
n. motive, motivation; adj. motivated

---

to suggest that something is true without saying so directly; to insinuate
*Although he didn't complain, his reaction **implied** that he was disappointed.*
n. implication; adj. implicit, implied

---

to show; to uncover
*The blinds were pulled up to **reveal** a beautiful view.*
n. revelation; adj. revealing

---

to put into effect; to enact
*We will **implement** a time-card system next year.*
n. implement, implementation

---

to flourish; to do well; to prosper
*She believes that Mike will **thrive** in his new job.*

strive
striving, strived/strove
verb

---

require
requiring, required
verb

---

accelerate
accelerating, accelerated
verb

---

respond
responding, responded
verb

---

reject
rejecting, rejected
verb

to try; to attempt or endeavor
*As a female CEO, Natalie **strives** to be a role model for other women in the industry.*
n. striver

---

to need or demand
*Reading this spreadsheet **requires** a lot of patience.*
n. requirement; adj. required

---

to gain speed; to speed up
*The gas pedal makes a car **accelerate**.*
n. acceleration

---

to answer; to reply
*It is likely that only half of the people we contact will **respond** to our survey.*
n. response, respondent, responsiveness adj. responsive

---

to refuse to accept; to dismiss
*Very few scientists entirely **reject** this theory.*
n. reject, rejection; adj. rejected

occasion
noun

---

factory
noun

---

vital
adjective

---

amiable
adjective

---

fluent
adjective

a specific time or event
*The store had to wait for the appropriate **occasion** to close for renovation.*
v. occasion; adj. occasional

---

a building that manufactures products
*The new business owners hadn't decided if they want to open their own **factory** or have their products made by others.*

---

1. necessary for life
2. of extreme importance
*1. Oxygen is **vital** for humans.*
*2. It is **vital** that we complete construction on the new factory before the end of the fiscal year.*
n. vitality; adv. vitally

---

friendly; pleasant
*Even when Xavier was under significant stress, he was always an **amiable** person.*
n. amiability, amiableness; adv. amiably

---

able to speak a language proficiently
*It did not take Esther long to become **fluent** in Spanish.*
n. fluency; adv. fluently

describe
describing, described
verb

passion
noun

exceed
exceeding, exceeded
verb

derive
deriving, derived
verb

invest
investing, invested
verb

to explain something
*When he went to court, he had to **describe** the event with as much detail as he could remember.*
adj. describable

---

a strong emotion
*She was very **passionate** about world peace.*

---

to go above and beyond
*His presentation **exceeded** all of their expectations.*
n. exceeder

---

to obtain (something) from a source
*They **derived** great satisfaction from seeing him smile when he opened the present.*
n. derivation, derivative; adj. derived, derivative

---

to put money or effort into something in the hope of receiving a benefit
*He made his fortune by **investing** in the stock market.*
n. investment, investor

investigate
investigating, investigated
verb

decline
declining, declined
verb

utilize
utilizing, utilized
verb

seek
verb

encounter
encountering, encountered
verb

to look closely at something in order to determine the truth; to examine
*The SEC is **investigating** the company's involvement in the insider-trading scandal.*
v. investigation, investigator; adj. investigative

---

1. to become lower or worse; to decrease or diminish
2. to choose not to do something; to refuse
*1. The price of gold is projected to **decline** next year.*
*2. If the seminar is held on a Thursday, I will have to **decline** the invitation.*
n. decline; adj. declining

---

to use
*Our system will **utilize** the most advanced technology.*
n. utilization, utility

---

to look for
*The company plans to **seek** applicants for their new job opening.*
seeking, sought
n. seeker

---

to meet; to face
*Plans for a new shopping mall always **encounter** opposition in the city council.*
n. encounter

involve
involving, involved
verb

anticipate
anticipating, anticipated
verb

modify
modifying, modified
verb

undergo
undergoing, underwent
verb

underlie
underlying, underlay
verb

to make (someone) a part of something
When I heard about the exciting new project, I told my manager I want to be **involved**.
n. involvement; adj. involved

---

to expect or look forward to
Experts **anticipate** *a major victory by the opposite party in this election.*
n. anticipation; adj. anticipated, anticipatory

---

to adapt; to change or adjust
She wants to **modify** *her car to run on solar power as well as gasoline.*
n. modification; adj. modified

---

to experience; to be subjected to
The website will **undergo** *a complete renovation.*

---

1. to be located beneath
2. to be a cause or reason for something
1. The layer of rock that **underlies** *the earth's crust is called the mantle.*
2. The fundamental issue that **underlies** *the conflict is her inexperience.*
adj. underlying

versatile
adjective

---

deduce
deducing, deduced
verb

---

credible
adjective

---

prevent
preventing, prevented
verb

---

inspire
inspiring, inspired
verb

having many functions
*She was **versatile** enough to take either position in the debate.*
n. versatility

to conclude; to determine
*After reviewing the security video footage, he was able to **deduce** who had taken the documents from his office.*
n. deduction, deducibility; adj. deducible

believable, trustworthy
*It is important to get your news from a **credible** source.*
n. credibility; adv. credibly

to stop something from happening
*He did his best to **prevent** the accident, but he could not stop the car in time.*
adj. preventable; n. preventability

to motivate or influence
*The speech **inspired** him to go home and write two more chapters.*
n. inspirer, inspiration; adv. inspiringly; adj. inspirational

refer
referring, referred
verb

---

aggression
noun

---

inquire
inquiring, inquired
verb

---

undertake
undertaking, undertook
verb

---

translate
translating, translated
verb

to direct attention or action towards something
*When she asked where she could find more information, the trainer **referred** her to the employee handbook.*
n. referral; adj. referable

---

hostility; a hostile action
*He was known for his **aggression** in meetings when he felt very strongly about something.*

---

to seek out information
*When Jon didn't show up for work, his boss called to **inquire** about his absence.*
n. inquirer, inquisition

---

to attempt; to take on (a task or job); to tackle
*They are **undertaking** a survey of the surrounding land.*

---

to interpret; to express in another language
*She loves to **translate** the plays of Shakespeare into other languages.*
n. translation, translator

terminate
terminating, terminated
verb

---

prohibit
verb

---

participate
participating, participated
verb

---

discriminate
discriminating, discriminated
verb

---

comprise
comprising, comprised
verb

to end; to bring or come to a close
*If the landlord **terminates** our lease, the entire office will have to relocate.*
n. termination

---

to forbid or ban
*Smoking is **prohibited** in this building.*
prohibiting, prohibited
n. prohibition; adj. prohibitive, prohibited

---

to take part in; to be involved in
*All employees are expected to **participate** in the company fundraiser.*
n. participation, participant; adj. participatory, participating

---

1. to treat differently because of prejudice
2. to detect differences, especially small or subtle ones; to differentiate or distinguish
1. *U.S. companies cannot **discriminate** against women and minorities in their hiring practices.*
2. *Newborn babies can't **discriminate** between different colors.*
n. discrimination; adj. discriminatory, discriminating

---

to be made up of; to consist of; to incorporate
*The United States of America **comprises** 50 individual states.*

consist
consisting, consisted
verb

vary
varying, varied
verb

rely
relying, relied
verb

substitute
substituting, substituted
verb

evaluate
evaluating, evaluated
verb

to be made up (of)
*This office **consists** of a president, a vice president, and 50 other employees.*

---

to change
*The town's population **varies** with the seasons, as many people have summer homes there.*
n. variation, variant, variance, variety; adj. various, variable, varied; adv. variously, variably

---

to be dependent (on something)
*I **rely** on my secretary to remind me when my next meeting is.*
n. reliance, reliability; adj. reliant, reliable; adv. reliably

---

to replace
*Jill needs to **substitute** the blue shirt for the red shirt in the ad.*
n. substitute, substitution

---

to assess, judge, or estimate
*An engineer plans to **evaluate** the condition of the house.*
n. evaluation

convene
convening, convened
verb

---

confide
confiding, confided
verb

---

diligence
noun

---

profile
noun

---

determine
determining, determined
verb

to assemble; to gather
*After working late into the night, the team decided to take a break and **convene** again in the morning.*

---

to share information openly
*She was so trustworthy, that everyone felt safe to **confide** in her.*
n. confider, confidence

---

significant effort put towards something
*Everyone was impressed by his **diligence**; he would not stop working until the project was completed.*
adv. diligently

---

compiled information about a person or thing
*Before she interviewed the candidate, she reviewed his **profile** in detail.*
v. profile

---

to decide based on information
*He was able to **determine** that he wanted the job after reading the job description.*
adj. determined

engage
engaging, engaged
verb

resolve
resolving, resolved
verb

cancel
canceling, canceled
verb

outgrow
outgrowing, outgrew
noun

appreciate
appreciating, appreciated
verb

to involve in
*He wanted to **engage** her in further conversation.*
adj. engaging

---

1. to make a decision
2. to find an answer to a problem
*1. She **resolved** to take another approach next time.*
*2. He **resolved** the supply issue by assigning the project to a less remote factory.*
n. resolver, resolution

---

to decide something will not happen; to stop from happening
*They had to **cancel** the business trip due to bad weather.*

---

to no longer need or be able to use (something) due to growth or development
*The company hopes that its international branch will soon **outgrow** its small offices.*

---

to be grateful for
*I really **appreciate** your generous help.*
n. appreciation; adj. appreciative, appreciable; adv. appreciatively, appreciably

monitor
monitoring, monitored
verb

construct
constructing, constructed
verb

establish
establishing, established
verb

conclude
concluding, concluded
verb

survive
surviving, survived
verb

to observe; to keep track of
*The accounting department is tasked with **monitoring** corporate spending.*
n. monitor; adj. monitored

---

to build or form
*The attorney needs to **construct** a convincing argument.*
n. construction, construct; adj. constructive, constructed

---

1. to set up; to found
2. to show that something is a fact
1. *This company was **established** in 1838.*
2. *The prosecutor can **establish** that the defendant was there at the time of the robbery.*
n. establishment; adj. established

---

1. to finish; to end
2. to develop a judgment after studying or considering something
1. *Each chapter **concludes** with a brief summary.*
2. *By the end of the meeting, we had **concluded** that your plan was best.*
n. conclusion; adj. conclusive, concluded, concluding; adv. conclusively

---

to last or live through an event or period of time; to endure
*Many companies did not **survive** the recession.*
n. survival, survivor; adj. surviving

recommend
recommending, recommended
verb

---

scrutinize
scrutinizing, scrutinized
verb

---

pollute
polluting, polluted
verb

---

simulate
simulating, simulated
verb

---

ensure
ensuring, ensured
verb

1. to advise
2. to say positive things about; to endorse
1. I **recommend** you revise the e-mail.
2. I will be happy to **recommend** you for the accounting position.
n. recommendation; adj. recommended

---

to closely inspect or examine
*The results were unexpected, but after **scrutinizing** the data, we determined that they were accurate.*
n. scrutiny

---

to contaminate or make unclean
*The river has been **polluted** by chemicals from the factory.*
n. pollution, pollutant; adj. polluted

---

to imitate; to mimic
*Astronauts train in water to **simulate** the experience of weightlessness.*
n. simulation, simulator; adj. simulated

---

to make certain; to guarantee
*We followed the schedule to **ensure** that we would complete the project on time.*

admit
admitting, admitted
verb

---

feasible
adjective

---

oblige
obliging, obliged
verb

---

productive
adjective

---

compete
competing, competed
verb

1. to confess
2. to allow; to permit
1. He **admitted** that he had plagiarized that section of the book.
2. The tickets **admit** two people to the demo fair.
n. admittance, admitter; adv. admittedly

---

able to occur; likely
The CEO decided that the plan was **feasible** given the progress the company had made.
n. feasibility; adv. Feasibly

---

to be required to do something (often in return for a favor)
I feel **obliged** to comply with her request because she always helps me.
n. obligation; adj. obligatory

---

to accomplish many things
He is always more **productive** when he eats breakfast.
n. productivity, productiveness

---

to try to win something
They **competed** for the grand prize in the company contest.
n. competition

satisfy
satisfying, satisfied
verb

---

character
noun

---

consequence
noun

---

commence
commencing, commenced
verb

---

approach
approaching, approached
verb

to meet the requirements or expectations
*It seemed that no matter what she did, she was unable to **satisfy** the board members.*
n. satisfaction; adj. satisfactory

the traits of a person
*It takes strength of **character** to admit that you failed.*

the result of an action
*You chose to cheat on the evaluation, so you will have to handle the **consequences** of that decision.*
adv. consequently

to begin
*Construction of the new building will **commence** next week.*
n. commencement

to come close to
*Temperatures are expected to **approach** record highs this summer.*
n. approach; adj. approachable

consult
consulting, consulted
verb

distract
distracting, distracted
verb

enable
enabling, enabled
verb

assess
assessing, assessed
verb

persist
persisting, persisted
verb

to seek advice or information from
*You should **consult** your lawyer before signing a contract.*
n. consultation, consultancy, consultant; adj. consultative

---

to divert or take away someone's attention
*The music can **distract** me from my work.*
n. distraction; adj. distracting

---

to make able or possible
*A new computer would **enable** us to work faster.*
n. enabler

To judge the nature, quality, or degree of (something); to evaluate or appraise
*The group was asked to **assess** the accuracy of information they found on the website.*
n. assessment, assessor; adj. assessable, assessed

---

to last; to go on; to endure
*The bad weather is expected to **persist** for another week.*
n. persistence; adj. persistent; adv. persistently

devote
devoting, devoted
verb

---

cease
ceasing, ceased
verb

---

doubt
doubting, doubted
verb

---

precede
preceding, preceded
verb

---

unify
unifying, unified
verb

to commit; to dedicate
*The founder and CEO has **devoted** his life to building this company.*
n. devotion, devotee; adj. devoted; adv. devotedly

---

to end; to conclude; to stop
*The construction on Market St. has finally **ceased**.*
n. cessation

---

to suspect of being untrue
*The police have begun to **doubt** her version of events.*
n. doubt; adj. doubtful; adv. doubtfully

---

to go or come before
*Twenty policemen on motorcycles **precede** the president's limousine on the way to the airport.*
n. precedent, precedence; adj. preceding

---

to bring or come together; to unite
*The two competing companies were **unified** in the merger.*
n. unification, unifier; adj. unified, unifying

effect
noun

dignity
noun

consider
considering, considered
verb

promise
promising, promised
verb

protect
protecting, protected
verb

result
*His speech had a positive **effect** on the listeners.*
adj. effective, effectible, effectual

---

worthy of honor
*She always treated everyone she met with **dignity** and respect.*

---

to think something over
*She **considered** his proposal carefully before making a decision.*
n. consideration

---

to commit to doing something
*He **promised** he would come to the office party.*
n. promise

---

to keep someone or something safe
*Her job was to **protect** the company's interests.*
n. protection; adv. protectively

reputation
noun

---

address
addressing, addressed
verb

---

gather
gathering, gathered
verb

---

insert
inserting, inserted
verb

---

deteriorate
deteriorating, deteriorated
verb

how someone is seen to others
*It was important to Kamala to have a good **reputation**.*
adj. reputable

---

to speak to
*He **addressed** his concerns to the president of the company.*
n. address

---

to bring together
*She knew she needed to **gather** more data.*
n. gathering, gatherer

---

to put (something) into something else
*To start the program, **insert** the driver and follow the instructions.*
n. insertion

---

to grow worse
*The patient's condition has **deteriorated** since last night.*
n. deterioration; adj. deteriorating

correspond

corresponding, corresponded
verb

cooperate

cooperating, cooperated
verb

dominate

dominating, dominated
verb

facilitate

facilitating, facilitated
verb

retain

retaining, retained
verb

1. to be very similar to something; to match almost exactly
2. to communicate in writing
1. *The Greek letter alpha **corresponds** with the letter "A" in the Roman alphabet.*
2. *I have **corresponded** with him for several months.*
n. correspondence, correspondent; adj. corresponding

---

to work together in order to accomplish something; to collaborate
*The team needs to **cooperate** in order to finish the project in time.*
n. cooperation; adj. cooperative; adv. cooperatively

---

to exert control over
*The project funding issues **dominated** the meeting.*
n. domination, dominance; adj. dominant

---

to make a process or activity easier
*This translation program can be used to **facilitate** language learning.*
n. facilitator, facilitation

---

to keep or hold
*It's important that the company **retain** its core values of customer service and integrity.*
n. retention, retainer; adj. retentive

complement

complementing, complemented
verb

---

compliment

complimenting, complimented
verb

---

occupy

occupying, occupied
verb

---

manipulate

manipulating, manipulated
verb

---

waive

waiving, waived
verb

to bring out the best in or supply a missing quality to; to be the ideal partner or accompaniment

*As a team, they **complement** each other well; she analyzes data, and he understands people.*

n. complement; adj. complementary

---

to make a positive comment about; to praise

*He **complimented** her excellent taste in music.*

n. compliment; adj. complimentary

---

1. to be in (a place or position); to inhabit
2. to engage, employ, or keep busy

1. *She has **occupied** the corner office for the past two years.*
2. *The toy can **occupy** the boy for hours.*

n. occupancy, occupant, occupier, occupation; adj. occupied

---

to influence or control

*One of the board members attempted to **manipulate** the results of the vote.*

n. manipulation, manipulator; adj. manipulative, manipulated;
adv. manipulatively

---

to give up; to relinquish

*He wants to **waive** his right to an attorney.*

n. waiver

veracity
noun

categorize
categorizing, categorized
verb

risk
noun

accommodate
accommodating, accommodated
verb

attend
attending, attended
verb

accuracy; truth
*Before you submit your resume, check the **veracity** of everything on the page to make sure no errors were overlooked.*

---

to characterize a group of items
*We have to **categorize** all the expenses as essential or non-essential by Friday.*
n. categorization, category

---

the possibility that something bad might occur
*It's important to assess the **risk** in your decisions.*
adj. risky

---

to make or provide room for
*Because she was given advance notice, she was able to **accommodate** the request.*
n. accommodation

---

to go to an event
*Although he wanted to **attend** the conference in Orlando, he was unable to get approval.*
n. attendance adj. attender

arrange
arranging, arranged
verb

access
accessing, accessed
verb

allocate
allocating, allocated
verb

convince
convincing, convinced
verb

perceive
perceiving, perceived
verb

to set up; to put in order
*She **arranged** the slides in the presentation.*
n. arrangement; adj. arranger

---

to gain entry to
*His badge allowed him to **access** the restricted floor of the building.*
n. access; adj. accessible

---

to set aside
*She examined the budget and **allocated** funds toward the project.*
n. allocation; adj. allocated

---

to cause (a person) to agree with a statement or opinion; to persuade
*I have to **convince** him that my decision is correct.*
adj. convincing, convinced; adv. convincingly

---

to sense; to be aware of
*Dogs **perceive** a greater range of sounds than humans do.*
n. perception; adj. perceived, perceptible; adv. perceptibly

attribute
attributing, attributed
verb

---

occur
occurring, occurred
verb

---

intimidate
intimidating, intimidated
verb

---

reinforce
reinforcing, reinforced
verb

---

pursue
pursuing, pursued
verb

to give credit or assign responsibility for (something) to a particular person, condition, etc.
*She **attributes** her recent promotion to hard work and a positive reputation.*
n. attribution, attribute; adj. attributable, attributed

---

to happen; to take place
*The meeting **occurred** last Wednesday.*
n. occurrence

---

to challenge (a person's) confidence; to make nervous or afraid
*His partner's knowledge is so wide that it sometimes **intimidates** him.*
n. intimidation; adj. intimidating

---

to make stronger or more intense
*She reads only books that **reinforce** her own beliefs.*
n. reinforcement; adj. reinforced

---

to follow or chase after
*It's important to **pursue** your professional goals.*
n. pursuit, pursuer

concentrate
concentrating, concentrated
verb

ignore
ignoring, ignored
verb

detect
detecting, detected
verb

expand
expanding, expanded
verb

clarify
clarifying, clarified
verb

to focus, to direct one's attention to
*My boss suggested that I **concentrate** on improving my public speaking skills.*
n. concentration

to pay no attention to
*He **ignored** the email and missed the meeting as a result.*
adj. ignored

to sense or discover something; to discern; to identify
*I could **detect** some uncertainty in her voice when she answered.*
n. detection, detective, detector; adj. detectable; adv. detectably

to move apart or outwards so as to take up more space; to grow
*Their territory **expanded,** which caused them to increase their workforce.*
n. expansion, expansionism; adj. expansive, expanding

to make something clearer or easier to understand; to explain
*The candidate had to **clarify** his statements about environmental policy.*
n. clarification, clarity; adj. clarified

incorporate
incorporating, incorporated
verb

position
noun

reduce
reducing, reduced
verb

physical
adjective

code
noun

1. to include
2. to form a group or corporation
1. His report **incorporates** all of the necessary components.
2. The entrepreneur decided she was ready to **incorporate** her business.
n. incorporation

---

situation or location
The GPS gave him the exact **position** of the restaurant he was looking for.
adj. positional

---

to minimize; to make smaller
She decided to **reduce** the number of employees in the home office.
n. reduction

---

having to do with a material trait
I am interested in the **physical** aspect of science.
adv. physically

---

1. a way of communication only a select group of people can understand
2. instructions for a computer
1. When sending defense plans, the military uses **codes** so that the messages won't be understood if they are intercepted.
2. Todd updated the payroll software's **code** so it could calculate bonuses based on how long each employee had been at the firm.
v. code; n. coder

glimpse
glimpsing, glimpsed
verb

practice
practicing, practiced
verb

verbal
adjective

permit
permitting, permitted
verb

justify
justifying, justified
verb

to catch sight of
*I caught a brief **glimpse** of the text message before it was deleted.*
n. glimpse, glimpser

to work on habitually
*When you are learning a new language, it is important to **practice** every day.*
n. practice

expressed in words
*The nurse required a **verbal** response before he could continue.*
adv. verbally; v. verbalize

to allow
*The company decided it could no longer **permit** employees to work from home.*
n. permission, permit; adj. permitted, permissive; adv. permissively

to show or claim that something is right or reasonable
*She tried to **justify** his theft by claiming the company owed her the money.*
n. justification; adj. justifiable, justified; adv. justifiably

fluctuate
fluctuating, fluctuated
verb

---

deviate
deviating, deviated
verb

---

export
exporting, exported
verb

---

import
importing, imported
verb

---

regulate
regulating, regulated
verb

to vary frequently and irregularly; to vacillate
*The temperature has been **fluctuating** a lot recently, so I wasn't sure if I should wear a coat.*
n. fluctuation; adj. fluctuating

---

to differ or stray from an established standard or course; to vary or diverge
*The final version of the building will **deviate** only slightly from the original plan.*
n. deviation, deviant; adj. deviant

---

to send something out of the country, usually for sale
*Their business will **export** dairy products to Europe.*
n. exporter, export, exporting; adj. exported

---

to bring something into the country, usually for sale
*He plans to **import** wine from Europe.*
n. importer, import, importing; adj. imported

---

to control, especially by making rules; to supervise
*The government **regulates** the sale of certain medicines.*
n. regulation, regulator; adj. regulatory, regulated

provide
providing, provided
verb

---

qualify
qualifying, qualified
verb

---

succeed
succeeding, succeeded
verb

---

remove
removing, removed
verb

---

commit
committing, committed
verb

to supply
*We will **provide** the data they need by Tuesday.*
n. provision, provider

---

to meet requirements; to be or become eligible
*Her score on the entrance exam **qualifies** her for the next step.*
n. qualification, qualifier; adj. qualified, qualifying

---

to achieve a goal
*He **succeeded** in getting his novel published.*
n. success; adj. successful; adv. successfully

---

to take (something) off or away
*She **removed** the paper that was stuck in the printer.*
n. removal; adj. removable

---

1. to promise to do something; to pledge
2. to carry out (a crime, etc.)
1. *We **committed** to working here until the end of the summer.*
2. *I never thought he would **commit** perjury.*
n. commitment; adj. committed

develop
developing, developed
verb

conference
noun

technical
adjective

abundant
adjective

accomplish
accomplishing, accomplished
verb

to grow
*Before she presented her idea to the corporation, she needed to **develop** it thoroughly.*
adj. developing; n. development

---

a meeting
*He decided to attend the **conference** in order to learn from other great speakers.*
adj. conferential

---

pertaining to the specialized or practical skills of science, art, or any particular profession
*The applicant knew about the field in general, but did not have any **technical** experience.*
adv. technically

---

more than enough
*The supply closet had **abundant** pens and rubber bands.*
n. abundance; adv. abundantly

---

to complete something, usually an achievement
*She was able to **accomplish** the homework assignment in half the time she thought it would take.*
n. accomplishment; adj. accomplished

able
adjective

apply
applying, applied
verb

confidence
adjective

exclude
excluding, excluded
verb

estimate
estimating, estimated
verb

capable; having the necessary resources
*He was surprised that he was **able** to lift the box; it was much lighter than it looked.*
n. ability

1. to use for a purpose
2. to make a request
1. *She **applied** her problem-solving skills to the project at hand.*
2. *He **applied** for a small business loan.*
n. application; adj. applicable

belief in yourself
*She had a large amount of **confidence** in her management skills.*
adj. confident

to leave out; to omit
*Rob didn't understand why there was data **excluded** from the report.*
n. exclusion; adj. exclusionary, exclusive, excluded; adv. exclusively

to make an educated guess
*We **estimate** that next year's profits will be 20 percent higher.*
n. estimate, estimation; adj. estimated

legislate

legislating, legislated
verb

---

indicate

indicating, indicated
verb

---

daunt

daunting, daunted
verb

---

founder

foundering, foundered
verb

---

goad

goading, goaded
verb

to make law
*Congress **legislated** a federal minimum wage in 1938.*
n. legislation, legislator, legislature; adj. legislative; adv. legislatively

---

to show or suggest
*Please fill out the form and check the box to **indicate** you've read the contract.*
n. indication, indicator; adj. indicative

---

to discourage; to intimidate
*He tried hard not to let the enormity of the situation **daunt** him.*
adj. daunting, daunted

---

to sink; to fall helplessly; to fail after a period of time
*Their working relationship began to **founder** after she was promoted.*
adj. foundering

---

to prod or urge
*Denise had to **goad** Leigh into finishing the project with her.*

riddle
riddling, riddled
verb

nettle
nettling, nettled
verb

ply
plying, plied
verb

edit
editing, edited
verb

straightforward
adjective

to make many holes in; to permeate
*The bag was **riddled** with holes.*

---

to irritate
*It **nettles** my colleague that I was friends with our boss in college.*

---

1. to use diligently; to engage
2. to join together
*1. Heath needs the latest model of computer to **ply** his trade as a video-game tester.*
*2. The weaver **plied** the fibers together to make a basket.*

---

to change and improve a piece of writing
*Your manuscript is strong, but you need to **edit** it.*
n. editor, edition; adj. editorial; adv. editorially

---

uncomplicated; simple
*An effective speech should be **straightforward** and have a clear point.*
n. straightforwardness; adv. straightforwardly

fertile
adjective

---

condition
noun

---

delete
deleting, deleted
verb

---

display
displaying, displayed
verb

---

duplicate
duplicating, duplicated
verb

able to produce offspring or crops
*The doctor confirmed that she was **fertile** and could start trying to conceive a child.*
n. fertility, fertileness; adv. fertilely

a state of being
*When he started his new job, he felt that his life **condition** had greatly improved.*
adj. conditional

to erase
*When her phone fell into a puddle, all of her contact information was **deleted**.*
n. deletion

to show
*He made a presentation to **display** all of the information he had gathered for the project.*
n. display

to make a copy
*She **duplicated** the records so she would have a copy if anything happened to the original.*
n. duplication

search
searching, searched
verb

---

durable
adjective

---

recur
recurring, recurred
verb

---

compare
comparing, compared
verb

---

react
reacting, reacted
verb

to look for
*People in cafes are always **searching** for outlets to plug their computers into.*
searching, searched
n. search

---

able to last through tough conditions; enduring
*His phone is incredibly **durable**; he has dropped it many times and it still works.*
n. durability

---

to happen repeatedly
*She invited me to a **recurring** meeting on Mondays.*

---

to make note of differences and similarities (between two or more things)
*They **compared** cell phone plans to find the best deal.*
n. comparison; adj. comparable; adv. comparably

---

to act in response to; to respond
*How did your boss **react** when you told him you were getting married?*
n. reaction; adj. reactionary, reactive

convey
conveying, conveyed
verb

combine
combining, combined
verb

distribute
distributing, distributed
verb

promote
promoting, promoted
verb

consume
consuming, consumed
verb

1. to communicate or express
2. to transport
1. *She tried to **convey** the seriousness of the situation, but they didn't seem to grasp it.*
2. *The boxes were **conveyed** to Boston by train.*
n. conveyance

---

to put together; to blend
*The merger **combines** two companies that are each profitable on their own.*
n. combination; adj. combined

---

to give out; to divide among a group
*We are going to **distribute** the money evenly among the three of us.*
n. distribution, distributor; adj. distributional

---

1. to support or publicize
2. to raise (someone) to a higher grade or position
1. *Authors often go on television talk shows to **promote** their new books.*
2. *Jay worked very hard at his job, hoping he would be **promoted**.*
n. promotion, promoter

---

1. to buy or use up
2. to eat or drink
1. *Americans **consume** 25 percent of the world's oil.*
2. *He **consumed** the entire pie in under ten minutes.*
n. consumer, consumption; adj. consuming

distort
distorting, distorted
verb

eliminate
eliminating, eliminated
verb

injure
injuring, injured
verb

deplete
depleting, depleted
verb

transform
transforming, transformed
verb

to depict something inaccurately
*Bill is known for **distorting** the truth.*
n. distortion; adj. distorted

---

to get rid of; to remove or exclude
*They **eliminated** a product from the group in order to streamline production.*
n. elimination

---

to hurt
*If you aren't careful, you can seriously **injure** yourself while lifting a heavy box.*
n. injury; adj. injurious, injured; adv. injuriously

---

to use up
*Some critics worry that we are rapidly **depleting** the world's oil supply.*
n. depletion

---

to change dramatically
*The cell phone market will be **transformed** with the release of our new model.*
n. transformation

society
noun

management
noun

network
networking, networked
verb

process
processing, processed
verb

replace
replacing, replaced
verb

community, organization, or group of people
*Technology has greatly improved modern **society**.*
adj. societal

---

1. A group in charge of directing others.
2. The act of taking responsibility over something
*1. She was told to bring her problems to **management**.*
*2. He showed his **management** skills by listening to her thoughtfully.*

---

to connect to a group of people, usually for professional purposes
*He always made sure to attend company dinners because it was a great way to **network**.*
n. network, networker

---

1. to think something over for understanding
2. to manufacture
*1. It took her a while to **process** what had happened.*
*2. The factory **processes** candy bars.*
n. process

---

to exchange for something new
*Josie needs to **replace** the color ink cartridge in the printer.*
n. replacement

skill
noun

---

software
noun

---

store
storing, stored
verb

---

generate
generating, generated
verb

---

focus
focusing, focused
verb

something one is good at
*Public speaking is one of his many **skills**.*
adj. skilled, skillful; adv. skillfully

---

a program designed to complete a task on a computer
*The new **software** automatically corrects any spelling and punctuation errors.*

---

to hold
*Susan was asked to **store** her purse in her desk during work hours.*
n. store, storage

---

to produce; to create
*Her latest article is expected to **generate** a lot of controversy.*

---

to direct one's attention to; to concentrate
*We need to **focus** on the problem of water pollution before it is too late.*
n. focus; adj. focused

identify
identifying, identified
verb

---

persuade
persuading, persuaded
verb

---

organize
organizing, organized
verb

---

tolerate
tolerating, tolerated
verb

---

guarantee
guaranteeing, guaranteed
verb

to determine who or what a person or thing is; to recognize
*Jackie asked the group to **identify** the cause of the leakage.*
n. identity, identification; adj. identifiable, identified

---

to convince
*The partners **persuaded** the board to let her go.*
n. persuasion; adj. persuasive; adv. persuasively

---

1. to put in order
2. to arrange
1. *I must **organize** my desk so I can find things more easily.*
2. *They are planning to **organize** a concert to benefit local charities.*
n. organization, organizer; adj. organized

---

to allow or endure
*My boss doesn't **tolerate** lateness.*
n. tolerance; adj. tolerant, tolerable; adv. tolerantly, tolerably

---

to promise or ensure
*Can you **guarantee** that this program will work on my computer?*
n. guarantee; adj. guaranteed

contribute
contributing, contributed
verb

coincide
coinciding, coincided
verb

contradict
contradicting, contradicted
verb

recover
recovering, recovered
verb

perpetuate
perpetuating, perpetuated
verb

to give or donate
*Everyone **contributed** twenty dollars for a wedding gift for Evelyn.*
n. contribution, contributor; adj. contributed, contributing

---

to happen at the same time
*My mom's visit in May **coincides** with the company meeting in Vegas.*
n. coincidence; adj. coincidental; adv. coincidentally

---

to oppose or challenge (a person or statement); to dispute
*He will **contradict** your version of the story.*
n. contradiction; adj. contradictory

---

to improve after experiencing a decline
*The economy **recovered** quickly after the recent recession.*
n. recovery; adj. recoverable

---

to cause (something) to last indefinitely; to sustain
*Advertisements like these **perpetuate** sexism in our society.*
n. perpetuity; adj. perpetual; adv. perpetually

convention
noun

---

streamline
streamlining, streamlined
verb

---

present
presenting, presented
verb

---

conduct
conducting, conducted
verb

---

mentor
mentoring, mentored
verb

1. meeting
2. a method or rule
1. *The dentists had their annual **convention** in New Orleans every year.*
2. *She used the standard naming **convention** when she found the new species.*
adj. conventional

to make something more efficient; to improve
*He was hired to find a way to **streamline** the company's production line.*
adj. streamlined

to show or demonstrate
*She **presented** the data at the national conference.*
n. presentation, presenter

to manage; to direct
*He **conducted** the entire operation without a hitch.*
n. conduct, conductor

to provide an example for; to teach; to influence
*She was happy to **mentor** the new intern.*
n. mentorship, mentor

aware
adjective

raise
raising, raised
verb

base
noun

preliminary
adjective

valuable
adjective

to know; to be cognizant
*He was **aware** of someone entering the room.*
n. awareness

---

to lift in height or status
*After she received her MBA, she was able to **raise** herself to heights she had never imagined before.*
b. raise

---

the bottom layer; the starting point
*Building a successful organization requires a stable **base**.*
v. base

---

coming before or done in preparation for something
*Before starting the program, you will need to take a **preliminary** course.*
n. preliminary

---

of great worth; expensive
*The discs contained very **valuable** information.*
v. value; n. value; adj. valued

reluctant
adjective

---

subtle
adjective

---

vague
adjective

---

consistent
adjective

---

equivalent
adjective

unwilling, not eager
*He got the promotion, but he is **reluctant** to move abroad for the position.*
n. reluctance; adv. reluctantly

---

delicate or understated, not obvious; not easy to notice
*Their presentations were similar, but there were **subtle** differences.*
n. subtlety; adv. subtly

---

unclear; imprecise; not specific
*I don't remember exactly what he looked like, but I have a **vague** memory.*
n. vagueness; adv. vaguely

---

1. unchanging; stable
2. compatible; in line with
1. *Our team must be **consistent** in delivering our message.*
2. *The results of the blood test were **consistent** with the diagnosis.*
n. consistency; adv. consistently

---

equal
*One gallon is **equivalent** to four quarts.*
n. equivalent, equivalence, equivalency; adv. equivalently

valid
adjective

---

widespread
adjective

---

rigid
adjective

---

ultimate
adjective

---

abstract
adjective

1. acceptable as true; reasonable; convincing
2. legally binding or effective; legitimate
1. *She made a very **valid** point about the risks of this investment.*
2. *He will leave the country soon, because his visa is only **valid** until next week.*
v. validate; n. validity, validation; adj. validated; adv. validly

---

affecting or existing in a large area; extensive; general
*The merger caused **widespread** panic among the employees.*

---

hard; stiff; unyielding
*There is a **rigid** policy against casual dress at our company.*
n. rigidity; adv. rigidly

---

1. eventual; final
2. ideal; best
1. *Her career started badly, but her talent and dedication ensured **ultimate** success.*
2. *The **ultimate** computer would never run out of memory.*
n. ultimate, ultimatum; adv. ultimately

---

based on ideas or general concepts rather than physical reality or specific events
*This aspect of economics seems very **abstract**, but it has important real-life applications.*
n. abstraction, abstract; adv. abstractly

associate
associating, associated
verb

---

compensate
compensating, compensated
verb

---

flexible
adjective

---

achieve
achieving, achieved
verb

---

likewise
adverb

to join; to unite
*I was warned not to **associate** myself with him because many people do not like him.*
n. associate; adj. associate

---

to offset; to pay back
*She assumed that the company would financially **compensate** her for her trouble.*
n. compensator, compensation

---

willing to compromise or bend
*He was usually strict when it came to travel routes, but this time he was **flexible**.*
n. flexibility

---

to accomplish something
*Her parents were very proud of all she was able to **achieve** at her new job.*
n. achievement

---

similarly; in the same way; also
*I started the application and instructed the intern to do **likewise**.*

approximately
adverb

---

hence
adverb

---

via
adverb

---

ignorant
adjective

---

extensive
adjective

close to but not precisely; nearly; about
Approximately *5 percent of Americans commute to work using public transportation.*
v. approximate; n. approximation; adj. approximate, approximated

---

as a result; therefore; consequently
The cost of the new office is a major expense; ***hence*** *the need for cutbacks.*

---

by way of
We flew back from Los Angeles ***via*** *Chicago.*

---

lacking in knowledge; unaware; uneducated
He knows a lot about computer programs, but when it comes to politics he is completely ***ignorant****.*
n. ignorance, ignoramus; adv. ignorantly

---

wide-reaching; broad; substantial
She has ***extensive*** *experience with a variety of computer systems.*
v. extend; n. extent; adv. extensively

universal
adjective

---

positive
adjective

---

visible
adjective

---

essential
adjective

---

enormous
adjective

applying to all people or situations
*Fear of the unknown is a **universal** human trait.*
n. universality; adv. universally

---

good; not negative
*The new rules should have a **positive** effect on office morale.*
adv. positively

---

able to be seen
*In the all-glass conference room, their argument was **visible**.*
n. visibility; adv. visibly

---

absolutely necessary; crucial
*It is **essential** that we follow all the steps carefully.*
n. essence; adv. essentially

---

immensely large; huge
*The new desk is **enormous** and does not fit in the office.*
n. enormousness; adv. enormously

domestic
adjective

final
adjective

accurate
adjective

external
adjective

internal
adjective

1. relating to the home or housework
2. existing, originating, or taking place within one's own country
1. *Women and men today are likely to share the burden of **domestic** tasks.*
2. *Voters tend to be more interested in **domestic** issues than in foreign affairs.*
n. domesticity, domestic; adv. domestically

---

last
*Tomorrow is the **final** day of the conference.*
v. finalize; n. finality, finalization, final; adv. finally

---

perfectly correct, without errors
*He always checks his bill before paying to make sure it is **accurate**.*
n. accuracy; adv. accurately

---

on or from the outside
*Because no one at the company was able to solve the problem, an **external** consultant was hired.*
v. externalize; n. externality, externalization; adj. externalized; adv. externally

---

on or from the inside
*Technologies such as ultrasounds enable doctors to examine **internal** organs without surgery.*
v. internalize; n. internality, internalization; adj. internalized; adv. internally

retire
retiring, retired
verb

---

asset
noun

---

accumulate
accumulating, accumulated
verb

---

efficient
adjective

---

primary
adjective

1. to withdraw; to go away to a more private place
2. to leave a job once an appropriate age has been reached.
1. *After a long morning, she **retired** to her office to take a break.*
2. *He was able to **retire** at the age of 63.*
n. retiree

---

a desirable quality; a valuable item
*She saw his leadership skills as an **asset** to their team.*

---

to collect together; to increase in number
*His long-term goal was to **accumulate** a large fortune.*
n. accumulation

---

streamlined
*She operated in such an **efficient** manner that she completed the task in half of the time allotted.*
n. efficiency; adv. efficiently

---

main; major; most important or significant
*Their **primary** objective was to deliver high-quality service.*
n. primacy; adj. prime; adv. primarily

apprehensive
adjective

mature
adjective

annual
adjective

isolated
adjective

mental
adjective

nervous; worried that something bad will happen
*He is **apprehensive** about the interview.*
n. apprehensiveness; adv. apprehensively

---

fully grown; aged; adult
*She has become much more **mature** since she went away to college.*
v. mature; n. maturity, maturation

---

occurring once each year; yearly
*I am due for my **annual** review with my boss.*
adv. annually

---

solitary; alone
*Leslie felt very **isolated** working in a cubicle.*
v. isolate; n. isolation, isolationism

---

relating to the mind; intellectual or psychological
*His strange behavior led doctors to suspect he was suffering from a **mental** illness.*
n. mentality; adv. mentally

ethical
adjective

---

relevant
adjective

---

prior
adjective

---

remarkable
adjective

---

beneficial
adjective

concerning or consistent with accepted moral standards; moral
*Many people believe it is not **ethical** to hire someone who is related to you.*
n. ethicality, ethic, ethics; adv. ethically

---

connected to what is being considered; pertinent; applicable
*The judge ruled that this information wasn't **relevant** to the case.*
n. relevance; adv. relevantly

---

preexisting; earlier
*Maria had been incredibly successful in her **prior** role.*

---

noteworthy; striking; extraordinary
*Since the new program began, there has been a **remarkable** increase in the number of applicants to the company.*
adv. remarkably

---

good; having a positive effect
*It would be **beneficial** for her to apply for the internship early.*
n. benefit; adv. beneficially

infinite
adjective

unique
adjective

secure
adjective

available
adjective

capable
adjective

endless; limitless; innumerable; so great as to be impossible to measure or count

*The universe is so immensely large that many consider it to be **infinite**.*

n. infinity; adv. infinitely

---

exceptional; special; one of a kind

*His style is unlike anyone else's; it is **unique**.*

n. uniqueness; adv. uniquely

---

safe; assured

*Jenny has felt very **secure** since the office installed metal detectors.*

v. secure; n. security; adv. securely

---

readily obtained; possible to get

*This chair is **available** in six different colors.*

n. availability

---

able to do something; competent

*Her prior work experience has made her more than **capable** of handling her job responsibilities.*

n. capability

profit
noun

inspect
inspecting, inspected
verb

desire
desiring, desired
verb

project
projecting, projected
verb

deceptive
adjective

a monetary gain or advantage
*The new clothing line is showing an incredible **profit** margin.*
v. profit; adj. profitable

---

to look over carefully
*Dustin always **inspected** the expense report carefully.*
n. inspection

---

to want something
*She **desired** a promotion, so she worked her hardest every day.*
n. desire; adj. desired

---

1. to put one's feelings on someone else
2. to extrapolate, to predict the effects of a trend
*1. He felt responsible for the incident, so he **projected** his negative attitude onto everyone he met that day.*
*2. During the meeting, she planned to **project** the company's earnings for the next 5 years.*
n. projection

---

misleading; giving a false impression
*The pictures were **deceptive**—the parking space was much smaller than it looked.*
v. deceive; n. deception; adv. deceptively

intrinsic
adjective

---

contemporary
adjective

---

complex
adjective

---

crucial
adjective

---

intermediate
adjective

deeply rooted; essential; inherent
*Freedom of expression is an **intrinsic** American value.*
adv. intrinsically

1. existing or happening at the same time
2. existing or happening in the present; modern
*1. His childhood was **contemporary** with the First World War.*
*2. The new office furniture was very **contemporary**.*
n. contemporary

difficult to understand; complicated
*The problem was too **complex** to be solved in a single meeting.*
n. complexity

extremely important; indispensable
*The helicopter is delivering **crucial** supplies to a remote hospital.*
adv. crucially

situated between two stages; in the middle
*Before moving on to the advanced level, I am going to try the **intermediate** level.*

glib
adjective

---

stoic
adjective

---

potential
noun

---

overview
noun

---

phenomenon
noun

said in an insincere manner; offhand; casual
*The sales pitch was too **glib** for his taste.*

---

indifferent to or unaffected by emotions
*Her last day was difficult, but she remained **stoic**.*
adv. stoically

---

ability or promise
*His mentor thinks he has the **potential** to be a world-class trainer.*
adv. potentially

---

a general survey
*This book offers an **overview** of the major developments in astronomy since the time of Galileo.*

---

something that exists or occurs, especially something remarkable; an occurrence; a wonder
*Working remotely is quickly becoming a widespread **phenomenon**.*
adj. phenomenal; adv. phenomenally
plural: phenomena

foundation
noun

evidence
noun

option
noun

insight
noun

logic
noun

the base that something is built on; basis; underpinning
*Customer service is the **foundation** of our company.*
adj. foundational

---

facts that support a theory or assertion
*Although many believed she was guilty, there wasn't enough **evidence** to prosecute her for the crime.*
adj. evident, evidential, evidenced; adv. evidently

---

a choice or possibility
*There are several different **options** for getting Internet access.*
adj. optional; adv. optionally

---

understanding or appreciation
*This book gave me greater **insight** into modern politics.*
adj. insightful; adv. insightfully

---

reason; rational thinking
*The problem has to be solved with **logic**.*
n. logician; adj. logical; adv. logically

contract
noun

---

recruit
recruiting, recruited
verb

---

fulfill
fulfilling, fulfilled
verb

---

compile
compiling, compiled
verb

---

rigorous
adjective

an agreement
*After the meeting, the secretary wrote up the **contract** that had been discussed.*
adj. contractible

---

to enlist or find new people
*She was told to **recruit** as many people for the position as she could.*
n. recruiter

---

to satisfy completely
*She had a very **fulfilling** career.*
n. fulfillment

---

to gather information
*He **compiled** the data necessary to run the reports.*
n. compilation

---

strict; demanding
*Hospitals must maintain **rigorous** standards of cleanliness.*
n. rigor; adv. rigorously

profound
adjective

---

coherent
adjective

---

passive
adjective

---

conceivable
adjective

---

sufficient
adjective

extremely intense, meaningful, or thoughtful
*She has a **profound** understanding of the plight of the poor.*
n. profundity; adv. profoundly

---

logical; reasonable and consistent
*He had a **coherent** argument so he was able to convince them.*
n. coherence; adv. coherently

---

not actively participating; inactive
*They weren't involved in the vandalism; they were just **passive** witnesses.*
n. passivity; adv. passively

---

able to be thought of; imaginable
*We used every **conceivable** method to raise money for the project.*
v. conceive; adv. conceivably

---

enough
*There was **sufficient** data to build the case.*
v. suffice; n. sufficiency; adv. sufficiently

rapid
adjective

---

adequate
adjective

---

intellectual
adjective

---

minuscule
adjective

---

intense
adjective

fast; quick
*The ambulance crew has to provide a **rapid** response in emergencies.*
n. rapidity; adv. rapidly

---

of as much quantity or quality as is needed; sufficient; enough
*The standard of her work is barely **adequate**.*
n. adequacy; adv. adequately

---

intelligent; relating to intelligence; academic; educated
*Because he enjoys to read, his conversations are usually very **intellectual**.*
n. intellect, intellectual; adv. intellectually

---

extremely small; minute; tiny
*Her office is **minuscule**.*

---

extreme; severe
*He has an **intense** stare that can make people uncomfortable.*
v. intensify n. intensity, intensification; adj. intensive, intensified;
adv. intensely, intensively

ambiguous
adjective

compatible
adjective

medical
adjective

automatic
adjective

familiar
adjective

able to be interpreted in more than one way; unclear
*We had a long debate over some **ambiguous** passages in the proposal.*
n. ambiguity, ambiguousness; adv. ambiguously

suitable for; able to work with
*Her style of management was not **compatible** with the new team.*
n. compatibility

relating to healthcare and the science of treating diseases
*My son wants to get a **medical** degree and become a doctor or nurse.*
v. medicate; n. medicine; adv. medically

operating or happening on its own; self-activating
*The lights are on an **automatic** timer, so they turn on every day at exactly 7:30 a.m.*
v. automate; n. automation; adj. automated; adv. automatically

1. acquainted; having knowledge of
2. well-known; friendly
*1. I've read many of his books, so I'm **familiar** with his theories.*
*2. It was good to see a **familiar** face after my long stay abroad.*
n. familiarity

negotiate
negotiating, negotiated
verb

---

bargain
noun

---

outstanding
adjective

---

reconcile
reconciling, reconciled
verb

---

normal
adjective

to make a deal or agreement
*She was able to **negotiate** for the salary she deserved.*
n. negotiator

---

an agreement in which at least one party feels it is getting a good deal
*They bought the smaller company for $1 million, which many thought was a **bargain**.*
n. bargainer

---

excellent; superior
*His work was so **outstanding** that he received an instant promotion.*
adv. outstandingly

---

to settle an argument or disagreement
*I am glad they were able to **reconcile** after all of these years.*
n. reconciliation

---

natural; consistent with what is expected
*Is it **normal** for Americans to receive only two weeks of vacation?*
v. normalize; n. normality, normalization; adj. normalized; adv. normally

integral
adjective

---

comprehensive
adjective

---

objective
adjective

---

temporary
adjective

---

significant
adjective

necessary in order for something to be complete; extremely important
*You are an **integral** part of this project; we couldn't do it without you.*
adv. integrally

---

complete; thorough
*With your **comprehensive** work history, you should be able to find another job quickly.*
adv. comprehensively

---

unbiased; unprejudiced
*We need an **objective** opinion on our project.*
n. objectivity; adv. objectively

---

lasting a short time
*This won't work forever; it's only a **temporary** solution.*
adv. temporarily

---

worthy of attention; important; remarkable
*There has been a **significant** increase in the annual number of work-related injuries.*
n. significance; adv. significantly

maximum
adjective

minimum
adjective

considerable
adjective

ethnic
adjective

legal
adjective

of the greatest possible amount or degree; most
*We have the **maximum** number of participants in our study.*
v. maximize; n. maximum, maximization; adj. maximal; adv. maximally

---

of the least possible amount or degree
*They set a **minimum** GPA of 3.5 for applicants to the honors program.*
v. minimize; n. minimum, minimization; adj. minimal; adv. minimally

---

great in amount or extent; sizable; substantial; significant
*We have had **considerable** gains in our market share this year.*
adv. considerably

---

cultural; united or defined by culture, tradition, or nationality
*The event was intended to promote understanding between members of different **ethnic** groups in our company.*
n. ethnicity; adv. ethnically

---

allowed by or relating to the law; lawful
*The **legal** age to work in the United State varies by state.*
v. legalize; n. legalization, legality; adj. legalized; adv. legally

previous
adjective

---

distinctive
adjective

---

contrary
adjective

---

stable
adjective

---

inevitable
adjective

prior
*Do you have any **previous** experience?*
adv. previously

---

characteristic; special; unique
*The copy machine makes a **distinctive** sound when it is jammed.*
n. distinction; adj. distinct; adv. distinctively, distinctly

---

opposite; contradictory; conflicting
*No matter what I say, you always argue the **contrary** position.*
n. contrary; adv. contrarily

---

unlikely to change or shift; secure
*Tenure is at an all-time low, and we need to build a more **stable** work force.*
v. stabilize; n. stability, stabilization; adv. stably

---

impossible to prevent; unavoidable
*She missed so many deadlines, it was **inevitable** that she would lose her job.*
n. inevitability; adv. inevitably

afford
affording, afforded
verb

---

merchandise
noun

---

conserve
conserving, conserved
verb

---

prepare
preparing, prepared
verb

---

obvious
adjective

to be able to
*Jeremy cannot **afford** to have any additional errors with the budget.*
adj. affordable

---

goods; inventory
*The store was running low on **merchandise** after the sale.*
n. merchandiser

---

to use the least amount of
*He tried his best to **conserve** water during the drought.*
n. conservation, conservationist

---

to get ready
*She **prepared** the food for the office party.*
n. preparation, preparer

---

easily seen or recognized; clear
*It was **obvious** that he was going to win.*
adv. obviously

mutual
adjective

---

brief
adjective

---

fundamental
adjective

---

random
adjective

---

rational
adjective

shared by or affecting both parties
*The partners made a **mutual** decision to terminate her employment.*
adv. mutually

---

short
*There will be a **brief** announcement before the news conference.*
n. brevity; adv. briefly

---

basic; essential; intrinsic
*Our employees have a **fundamental** right to be treated with dignity and respect.*
n. fundamental; adv. fundamentally

---

without order or organization
*The seating assignments were **random**.*
n. randomness; adv. randomly

---

reasonable; logical
*A good judge must be **rational** and not easily swayed by emotion.*
v. rationalize; n. rationality, rationalization, rationalist; adv. rationally

similar
adjective

incredible
adjective

predominant
adjective

liable
adjective

identical
adjective

resembling something else; alike
*Their offices are **similar** but Nora's is a bit larger.*
n. similarity; adv. similarly

---

hard to believe; amazing; remarkable
*He has an **incredible** ability to learn new languages quickly.*
adv. incredibly

---

strongest or most prevalent; foremost; main; primary
*After the merger, the **predominant** feeling in the office is trepidation.*
v. predominate; n. predominance; adv. predominantly

---

legally responsible
*The company is **liable** for all damages.*
n. liability

---

exactly the same
*We hoped the other airline would be cheaper, but the ticket prices were **identical**.*
adv. identically

neutral
adjective

---

appropriate
adjective

---

global
adjective

---

mediocre
adjective

---

mandatory
adjective

belonging to neither of two opposing categories; impartial; unaffiliated
*The supervisor listened to both parties and remained **neutral**.*
v. neutralize; n. neutrality, neutralization; adj. neutralized; adv. neutrally

---

proper or suitable
*Her outfit was **appropriate** for work.*
n. appropriateness; adv. appropriately

---

relating to or affecting the entire world; widespread
*After years of operating locally, we have decided to become a **global** company serving people in many countries.*
n. globe, globalization; adv. globally

---

of moderate quality or ability; unexceptional; passable
*His job performance was **mediocre** at best.*
n. mediocrity

---

required; obligatory; compulsory
*Before their first day, employees must attend a **mandatory** orientation.*

supply
supplying, supplied
verb

---

discount
discounting, discounted
verb

---

realistic
adjective

---

yield
yielding, yielded
verb

---

statistic
noun

to provide something
*The company is able to **supply** its employees with health insurance.*
n. supplier, supply

---

to reduce the price
*The store will **discount** any shirt that has been on the shelf longer than three months.*
adj. discountable

---

possible; similar to real life
*It is not **realistic** to expect a promotion in the first two months.*
adv. realistically

---

to provide; to produce
*The field **yielded** far more crops than the farmer was expecting.*
n. yield

---

information derived from numerical analysis
*The latest **statistics** show an increase in employee tenure.*
n. statistician; adj. statistical; adv. statistically

publication
noun

---

error
noun

---

method
noun

---

revolution
noun

---

commerce
noun

1. the act of publishing a text
2. a published book, journal, magazine, etc.
1. *He is excited about the* **publication** *of his first novel.*
2. *She has written articles for several different* **publications**.

---

a mistake
This report contains an unacceptable number of **errors**.
v. err; adj. erroneous; adv. erroneously

---

a way of doing something; a technique
They are developing a new **method** *for learning to read music.*
n. methodology; adj. methodical, methodological; adv. methodically, methodologically

---

1. a circular movement; a rotation or turn
2. a dramatic change, especially the overthrow of a government
1. *Earth completes a* **revolution** *around the sun approximately every 365¼ days.*
2. *Political* **revolutions** *took place around the world in 2013 and 2014.*
v. revolve, revolutionize; n. revolutionary, revolt; adj. revolutionary

---

economic activity; trade; business
The new policies are supposed to encourage **commerce** *by helping small businesses.*
adj. commercial; adv. commercially

administration
noun

conflict
noun

partner
noun

innovation
noun

finance
noun

1. the group of people responsible for managing a company, government, etc.; management
2. the act of administering
*1. The proposal has to be approved by the **administration**.*
*2. He is going to business school to get a degree in **administration**.*
v. administer, administrate; n. administrator; adj. administrative; adv. administratively

---

a state or incident of disagreement or hostility; a clash
*There is often a **conflict** between one's personal desires and the best interest of the organization.*
v. conflict; adj. conflicting, conflicted

---

one who shares an activity, business, etc.
*Greg's business **partner** liquidated the fund.*
n. partnership

---

a new way of doing something; an invention
***Innovation** is the key to keeping the company competitive.*
v. innovate; n. innovator; adj. innovative; adv. innovatively

---

1. the field of banking and investments
2. (in plural) a person's or company's situation with respect to money
*1. My brother is a stockbroker, and I also plan to have a career in **finance**.*
*2. My **finances** are very bad right now, and I am afraid the bank will reject my loan application.*
v. finance; n. financier, financing; adj. financial; adv. financially

behavior
noun

prerequisite
noun

phase
noun

wisdom
noun

candidate
noun

the way that a person acts; conduct
*Her tardiness and general **behavior** have been unacceptable.*
v. behave; adj. behavioral; adv. behaviorally

something that must be done beforehand; a requirement or precondition
*An internship is a **prerequisite** to obtaining a job at my firm.*
adj. prerequisite

a stage
*The first **phase** of the renovation has already begun.*

knowledge and good judgment based on experience; good sense
*The decision demonstrated his **wisdom**.*
adj. wise; adv. wisely

a person seeking a position, especially a person running for election to public office
*She is one of three **candidates** for the director role.*
n. candidacy

balance
balancing, balanced
verb

borrow
borrowing, borrowed
verb

collaborate
collaborating, collaborated
verb

agenda
noun

status
noun

to be equal; to arrange
*Melanie worked to **balance** her career and personal life.*
n. balance; adj. balanceable

---

to take with the intention of returning
*He often went to the library so that he could **borrow** books.*
n. borrower, adj. borrowable

---

to work together
*The finance team **collaborated** with the IT team to come up with a profitable solution.*
n. collaboration

---

a plan; an outline of events
*She was required to make an **agenda** before each meeting.*

---

1. importance in relation to others; rank
2. condition or state
1. *People often judge the social **status** of others based on the way they dress.*
2. *Eva asked for the **status** of the report, so she would know how close it was to completion.*

ideology
noun

location
noun

controversy
noun

incentive
noun

outcome
noun

a strong and rigid system of belief; dogma
*Communist **ideology** was influential during the twentieth century.*
n. ideologue; adj. ideological; adv. ideologically

---

a position or site; a place
*They still haven't found a good **location** for the new factory.*
v. locate; adj. located

---

intense public disagreement about something; a debate
*A **controversy** arose over the appointment of the new vice president.*
adj. controversial; adv. controversially

---

a reward for doing something
*To attract new clients, the sales team is offering additional **incentives**.*

---

a result
*The **outcome** of the election was a surprise to everyone.*

proficiency
noun

instance
noun

gender
noun

concept
noun

diversity
noun

ability; skill; competence
*Applying for a job in another country requires demonstration of language **proficiency**.*
adj. proficient; adv. proficiently

---

an example of an action or phenomenon; an occurrence; an occasion
*It was just one more **instance** of personal success.*

---

the sex of a person
*Discrimination based on **gender** is illegal in the United States.*
adj. gendered

---

an idea, especially one that is abstract and general
*As an introduction, he explained the major **concepts** that would be covered in the class.*
v. conceptualize; n. conception, conceptualization; adj. conceptual, conceptualized; adv. conceptually

---

variety, especially in terms of culture or ethnicity
*The **diversity** of the workforce has increased significantly in the past decade.*
v. diversify n. diversification adj. diverse, diversified adv. diversely

leeway
noun

resource
noun

proof
noun

opportunity
noun

alternative
noun

flexibility; freedom; room for variation or to maneuver
*Janice gave the new hire a lot of **leeway** for mistakes.*

---

a stock of information, skill, money, etc., that can be used to make or accomplish something
*Do you have enough **resources** to carry out this project?*
adj. resourceful

---

evidence showing that a statement or fact is true; verification
*New customers are required to show **proof** that they live in the neighborhood.*
adj. verified

---

a chance to do something
*The presentation will give her an **opportunity** to demonstrate her talent.*
adj. opportune; adv. opportunely

---

any of multiple options; another possibility
*We will explore several **alternatives** to the first proposed solution.*
adj. alternative; adv. alternatively

forecast
forecasting, forecast/forecasted
verb

lobby
lobbying, lobbied
verb

repel
repelling, repelled
verb

uniform
adjective

trend
noun

to predict
*The weather was **forecast** a week ahead of time.*
n. forecast, forecaster; adj. forecasted

---

to attempt to influence
*The protestors were using their signs to **lobby** their congressmen.*
n. lobbyer, lobbyist

---

to drive away
*They were **repelled** by the car dealer's behavior.*
n. repellant

---

consistent; the same
*It was crucial that each person completed the task in a **uniform** manner.*
n. uniformity

---

a dominant pattern or direction; a tendency
*The upward **trend** of employee engagement is continuing.*
v. trend; adj. trendy

function
noun

comment
noun

lecture
noun

emphasis
noun

analysis
noun

what something is used for; purpose or utility
*It is important that you understand the **function** of the machine.*
v. function; n. functionality; adj. functional, functioning; adv. functionally

---

a remark that expresses an observation or opinion
*We never had a chance to give our **comments** on the proposal.*
v. comment; n. commentary, commentator

---

a speech intended to teach something
*Are you interested in attending the **lecture** on women in the workplace?*
v. lecture; n. lecturer

---

special attention; stress; prominence
*The new laws put an **emphasis** on protecting the environment.*
v. emphasize; adj. emphatic; adv. emphatically
plural: emphases

---

a detailed interpretation of information
*An **analysis** of the test results showed gradual improvement in customer satisfaction.*
n. analyst; v. analyze; adj. analytical, analyzed; adv. analytically
plural: analyses

hypothesis
noun

circumstance
noun

strategy
noun

tradition
noun

regime
noun

an unproven theory, especially a scientific one
*Her **hypothesis** was that the new project management tool would increase efficiency.*
v. hypothesize; adj. hypothetical; adv. hypothetically
plural: hypotheses

a condition or fact that affects an event or creates a situation
*The room was cold and dark, and she hadn't slept the night before; it is difficult to take a test under those **circumstances**.*
adj. circumstantial

a plan for how to do something; a method
*It is important that we devise a **strategy** for the project.*
v. strategize; n. strategist; adj. strategic; adv. strategically

a practice or belief that has existed for a long time; a custom
*Our office **tradition** is to take new hires to lunch on their first day.*
n. traditionalist; adj. traditional; adv. traditionally

a government, usually one that is oppressive and authoritarian
*His book discusses the various groups that opposed the Nazi **regime**.*

target
noun

---

era
noun

---

authority
noun

---

generation
noun

---

hierarchy
noun

something that is aimed for; a goal
*To meet our **target**, we have to increase sales by 15 percent.*
v. target; adj. targeted

---

a long period in history that has defining characteristics
*She recommended a book about the colonial **era**.*

---

the power or right to make decisions or judgments about something
*The executive director is the final **authority** on the matter.*
adj. authoritative; adv. authoritatively

---

all of the people who are born within a particular period of time
*The current **generation** of college graduates is much more comfortable with technology.*

---

a fixed order of things by status or importance
*The secretaries have a **hierarchy** based on seniority.*
adj. hierarchical; adv. hierarchically

transaction
noun

---

audit
noun

---

examine
examining, examined
verb

---

unison
noun

---

topic
noun

deal; bargain
*The **transaction** took place on Wednesday.*
adj. transactional

an official examination
*The business was prepared for an **audit** at any time.*
v. audit; adj. audited

to look at thoroughly
*The scientist **examined** the specimen before making any classifications.*
n. examination

at the same time
*They always spoke in **unison**.*

a subject for study or discussion
*The **topic** of the staff meeting was employee morale.*
adj. topical; adv. topically

principle
noun

---

boon
noun

---

fracas
noun

---

policy
noun

---

consequently
adverb

an idea that forms the foundation of a theory or of a system of morality
*The **principle** of equality is an important part of any true democracy.*
adj. principled

---

blessing; something to be thankful for
*Dirk realized that his new coworker's computer skills would be a real **boon** to the company.*

---

noisy dispute
*When the players discovered that the other team was cheating, a violent **fracas** ensued.*

---

a procedure for dealing with something
*The administration is developing a new **policy** on immigration.*

---

as a result; for this reason; therefore; accordingly
*Business was down; **consequently**, they laid off 10% of the staff.*
n. consequence adj. consequent

subsequently
adverb

---

definitely
adverb

---

nevertheless
adverb

---

initially
adverb

---

furthermore
adverb

following this; later; afterwards; thereafter
She retired from her banking job at age 65 and **subsequently** *became involved in charity work.*
adj. subsequent

---

certainly; assuredly
He **definitely** *will be disciplined for making personal phone calls on the job.*
adj. definite, definitive; adv. definitively

---

in spite of that; nonetheless
Educational opportunities for women were limited in the nineteenth century; **nevertheless***, women were at the forefront of that era's scientific accomplishments.*

---

in the beginning; to begin with; at the start
The cost of the company party turned out to be much higher than we **initially** *expected.*
adj. initial

---

in addition; additionally; moreover
He was a great hire; **furthermore***, I believe he will run the company someday.*

overall
adverb

eventually
adverb

recently
adverb

chiefly
adverb

thereby
adverb

on the whole; in general
*Rebecca is a strong candidate, but I think Josh is a better candidate **overall**.*

---

in the end; ultimately
*He can only say a few words now, but **eventually** he will be able to speak fluently.*
n. eventuality; adj. eventual

---

in the not too distant past; not long ago
*The company has always offered benefits; however, we **recently** started offering free food.*
adj. recent

---

mostly; mainly; primarily
*The company's products were **chiefly** focused on social media.*
adj. chief

---

in this way; as a result of this
*Joe was the lead salesperson for the last two quarters and **thereby** earned a generous bonus.*

joint
adjective

---

profuse
adjective

---

goal
noun

---

progress
progressing, progressed
verb

---

majority
noun

something that is shared
*They moved forward with **joint** partnership.*
n. joint

---

something done freely or abundantly
*His apology was **profuse**; he kept repeating himself over and over again.*
adv. profusely; n. profuseness

---

the desired result
*She always sets realistic **goals** for herself.*

---

making forward motion
*As long as he **progressed** toward his goal each day, he was confident he would reach it.*
n. progression

---

the largest part of a whole; over half
*She held the **majority** of the shares as a 51% stockholder.*

minority
noun

---

talent
noun

---

data
noun

---

media
noun

---

narrative
noun

1. a small part of a whole; less than half
2. a member of a group that accounts for less than half of a population
1. Atheists are a **minority** in the United States.
2. The company is recruiting **minorities** for positions on its board of directors.

---

skill or ability
He has an amazing **talent** for working with our customers.
adj. talented

---

information
The report is based on **data** collected over a 25 year span.
singular: datum

---

news and entertainment outlets such as newspapers, television, radio, and film
The politician was happy with the way she had been depicted in the **media**.
singular: medium

---

a story; an account of connected events
The Odyssey is a long **narrative** in the form of a poem.
v. narrate; n. narration; adj. narrative; adv. narratively

tactic
noun

symbol
noun

duration
noun

expert
noun

labor
noun

a plan or technique for achieving a goal; a strategy
*The new **tactic** introduced by our boss helped us win the bid.*
n. tactician; adj. tactical; adv. tactically

---

an image, etc., that represents something else; a sign
*Many felt that the president stepping down was a **symbol** of the company's downfall.*
v. symbolize; n. symbolism; adj. symbolic; adv. symbolically

---

the length of time that something lasts
*Jon was on his phone for the **duration** of the meeting.*

---

a person who has special knowledge or experience in a particular field
*Jane is our resident computer **expert**.*
n. expertise; adj. expert; adv. expertly

---

work, especially physical work
*Companies must abide by the many laws governing **labor**.*
v. labor; adj. laborious; adv. laboriously

bias
noun

decade
noun

genre
noun

perspective
noun

text
noun

an attitude that is unfairly positive or negative about a particular group,
person, or thing in comparison to others; prejudice
*The company is accused of **bias** against the elderly in its hiring practices.*
adj. biased

a period of ten years
*The last **decade** has been financially difficult for the majority of the country.*

a style or category, especially a type of literature, etc.
*He prefers books in the **genre** of science fiction.*

a point of view
*I'd like to hear your **perspective** on this issue.*

a piece of writing
*There are several **texts** you are required to read before the conference.*
adj. textual

supervise
supervising, supervised
verb

fund
funding, funded
verb

respond
responding, responded
verb

dedicate
dedicating, dedicated
verb

income
noun

to oversee or manage
*Even though it was not his responsibility, he took on the task of **supervising** operations.*
adj. supervised

---

to provide money for
*The company **funded** a small get-together for a local pet shelter.*
n. fund; adj. funded

---

to answer
*She always made sure to **respond** to emails as soon as she read them.*
n. response

---

to devote
*He **dedicated** his life to world peace.*
n. dedication

---

money that is paid to a person or company; salary; earnings
*If she gets promoted, her **income** will increase substantially.*

assumption
noun

---

priority
noun

---

summary
noun

---

structure
noun

---

theory
noun

a belief that is not based on proof
*My calculations are based on the **assumption** that the costs will remain the same.*
v. assume; adj. assumed

something considered to be of the highest importance
*The main **priority** of the CFO is to drive results.*
v. prioritize; n. prioritization

a short description of the content of a longer piece of writing, film, etc.
*We were asked to write a one-page **summary** of the book.*
v. summarize; n. summarization; adj. summarized

1. the way in which the parts of something are put together; organization
2. a building or construction
1. *The **structure** of a basic proposal must include a time line.*
2. *The new office **structure** is a group of small buildings.*
v. structure; adj. structural, structured; adv. structurally

a system of ideas that is meant to explain a complex phenomenon; a belief, thesis, or hypothesis
*Scientists are developing new **theories** about the nature of the universe.*
v. theorize; n. theorist; adj. theoretical; adv. theoretically

revenue
noun

appearance
noun

climate
noun

research
noun

impact
noun

income; money that is earned
*The store had much higher **revenues** this year.*

---

the way something looks
*Heidi has a very professional **appearance**.*
v. appear; adj. apparent; adv. apparently

---

weather conditions over a long period of time; the environment
*Scientists are studying the forces causing changes in the **climate**.*
adj. climatic

---

intensive study of a particular topic
*He is doing **research** on women in business.*
v. research; n. researcher

---

an impression; an effect
*My discussion with the owner of the business had a great **impact** on me.*
v. impact; adj. impacted

challenge
noun

individual
noun

region
noun

sequence
noun

exception
noun

1. a difficult task or undertaking
2. a questioning of authority
1. *Employee tenure is our greatest **challenge** to overcome.*
2. *The new intern continued to **challenge** the supervisor in the meetings.*
v. challenge; n. challenger; adj. challenging, challenged

---

a single person
*She wanted to be recognized for her accomplishments as an **individual** instead of as a member of the group.*
n. individuality, individualism, individualist; adj. individual, individualistic, individualized; adv. individually

---

a large area that is considered to have unifying characteristics
*The southwestern **region** of the United States is known for its desert climate.*
adj. regional; adv. regionally

---

order
*The numbers in the code have to be entered in the right **sequence**.*
v. sequence; adj. sequential, sequenced; adv. sequentially

---

something that is not like others of its type; an anomaly
*Most people don't become millionaires in their twenties, but Selena is an **exception** to that rule.*
adj. exceptional; adv. exceptionally

spur of the moment

elephant in the room

with child

grandfathered in

push the envelope

spontaneously or impulsively; without prior planning
*The company picnic was supposed to be on Saturday, but the boss made a **spur of the moment** decision to change it to Sunday based on the weather forecast.*

Something that is very apparent that no one is talking about
*The meeting lasted 45 minutes before anyone acknowledged the **elephant in the room**.*

---

pregnant
*She didn't drink at the office party because she is **with child**.*

Something that is prohibited by new rules, but is allowed to continue because it existed before the rules went into effect.
*While the new vacation policy allows employees only two weeks of vacation a year, those hired before 2012 are **grandfathered in**, and may continue to take three*

---

to do something new and different that goes beyond what was previously thought to be possible; to innovate
*His new website really **pushes the envelope** of what the Internet can be used for.*

abide by the rules

carry on doing something

test the waters

pan out

account for a discrepancy

to accept and follow (a law, ruling, etc.); to comply with
*Both companies claim the right to sell the product, but they will **abide by** the judge's decision.*

to continue
*They will **carry on** with the meeting even though five people are absent.*

to check the impact of something before proceeding
*Before ancing their new initiative, the politicians **tested the waters** by conducting polls to assess the likely public response.*

to yield good results; to turn out well
*She has had several job interviews but nothing has **panned out** yet.*
[from *to pan for gold:* to attempt to extract gold from a river]

to explain; to provide an explanation for
*The police asked him to **account for** the missing money.*

give it away

---

follow suit

---

grow out of something

---

back up data

---

know the ropes

to reveal (information that was supposed to be kept secret)
*The party was supposed to be a surprise, but my boss **gave it away**.*

---

to do the same; to follow the example set by someone else
*She decided to skip the meeting and the rest of the team **followed suit**.*
[a reference to card games in which all players must play a card of the same suit as the one led by the first player]

---

1. to become too large for (something); to outgrow
2. to develop on the basis of (something)
1. *She gives her son's clothes to charity when he **grows out of** them.*
2. *This book **grew out of** a series of lectures I gave last year.*

---

to make an electronic copy (of a computer file, etc.) as security in case the original is damaged or deleted
*The power outage wasn't a problem because we had already **backed up** the files on the computer.*

---

to understand how things are done in a particular place
*To succeed in a new job, ask someone who really **knows the ropes** to train you.*
Hence, to **show someone the ropes** means "to show someone how things are done."
[a reference to sailing ships, which had complicated ropes and riggings]

back someone **into a corner**

---

second thoughts

---

look after someone

---

look forward to an event

---

look into something

to put (someone or oneself) into a position where there is no way out and no room to maneuver
*She has **backed** herself **into a corner** by setting the standards so high that no one—including her—can meet them.*

to reconsider
*After his first day on the job, he had **second thoughts** about taking the position.*

to take care of
*I asked Celia to **look after** the new hire.*

to anticipate (something) with pleasure
*I'm **looking forward to** the conference next week.*

to investigate; to seek information about
*We are **looking into** buying a new computer for the break room.*

cut a person **some slack**

---

first-rate

---

off base

---

touch base with

---

keep one's **options open**

to give someone a break; to be understanding
*My boss knew that I was going through a hard time, so when I missed the deadline, she **cut** me **some slack**.*

of high quality
*The accommodations in that hotel were **first-rate**.*

missing the point; not understanding
*I don't think he watched the news program properly; the conclusions he drew were way **off base**.*

check in with
*Even if my manager is having a busy week, she always makes time to **touch base with** me and catch up on my project work.*

to avoid doing anything that might rule out a future course of action
*He was unsure if the job was a good fit, so he decided to **keep** his **options open**.*

bring the facts **home** to someone

---

bring new information **to light**

---

see the light

---

look up

---

look something **up**

to make (the reality of something) clear
*This book finally **brought** the complexity of the issue **home** to me.*

---

to reveal; to uncover
*Their study **brought to light** some long-forgotten issues.*

---

to finally realize something after serious consideration
*I thought she would never agree with me, but eventually she **saw the light**.*

---

to show signs of improvement
*The most recent sales numbers are **looking up**.*

---

to seek information about (something) in a reference work
*I **looked up** the words that I didn't know in a dictionary.*

look up to someone

---

give someone **free rein**

---

rein someone **in**

---

give someone **the benefit of the doubt**

---

hold one's **own**

to have respect and admiration for (someone)
*He had always **looked up to** his uncle, who was an executive in the firm.*

---

to put few restrictions on the behavior of (someone)
*She has had **free rein** in the marketing department since her recent promotion.*
[A rein is the strap used to control a horse while riding; if loosened or freed, the horse can go as it wishes.]

---

to control (someone's) behavior closely
*Whenever he began to stray from the task, our supervisor **reined** him **in**.*

---

to assume that (a person or statement) is truthful until proven otherwise
*Her alibi is suspicious, but let's **give** her **the benefit of the doubt** until we know more.*

---

to perform reasonably well in a challenging situation
*Although he is the youngest one in the group, he is really **holding** his **own**.*

hold one's **tongue**

---

bring something to **mind**

---

set the record straight

---

use up a resource

---

size up the competition

to stay silent; to refrain from speaking
*She was upset and wanted to say something, but she **held** her **tongue**.*

---

to be reminiscent of (something); to remind
*That question **brings to mind** a recent conversation I had with my boss.*

---

to correct a false story; to provide accurate information
*On his last day, he wanted to **set the record straight** about why he was leaving.*

---

to consume (something) completely
*Who **used up** the ink cartridge and didn't replace it?*

---

to evaluate or assess
*The dogs growled and walked in a circle, **sizing** each other **up**.*

back down

---

back off

---

seeing things

---

second nature

---

have one's **hands tied**

to give up; to walk away from
*She always had to prove how smart she was; she never **backed down** from an argument.*

leave alone; let it be
*He is having a rough time; you should **back off**.*

seeing something that is not really there
*I could have sworn I saw her walk into her room 10 minutes ago, although I could be **seeing things**.*

something that comes easily without thought
*After Nicky gave birth, taking care of her son was **second nature** to her.*

to be restricted; to be prevented from doing something
*I wish I could give you more information, but my **hands are tied**.*

lower the bar

flare up

ask after someone

lost it

go through with something

to reduce standards so that it is easier to succeed
When no one qualified under the original criteria, the hiring committee **lowered the bar.**

---

to erupt or break out; to recur
With the stress from my new job, my ulcer **flared up** *again.*

---

to inquire about the well-being of (someone)
He heard your mother was in the hospital and called to **ask after** *her.*

---

react in an uncontrolled manner
When he heard the new employee received the promotion instead of him, he **lost it.**

---

to perform (an action) as planned; to carry out
We **went through with** *our plan to hold the meeting in spite of their absence.*

end up

lay claim to property

cross one's **mind**

hold on to

hold out

to come eventually to a particular situation or place
*It **ended up** costing much more than we expected.*
*After talking for hours, they **ended up** in the same place they started.*

to assert that one has the right to (something); to claim ownership of
*The new manager **laid claim to** the corner office.*

to occur to one
*I'm so accustomed to flying that the possibility of driving home never **crossed my mind**.*

to keep or retain
*She considered selling her shares, but she decided to **hold on to** them.*

to resist or endure in a challenging situation
*They offered him a reasonable salary, but he decided to **hold out** for a higher one.*

leave no stone unturned

---

cross paths

---

run into someone

---

have one's **work cut out for**

---

get one's **act together**

to look everywhere; to attempt everything
*We **left no stone unturned** in our search for the best location.*

---

to meet by chance
*They **crossed paths** in Las Vegas, where they both happened to be attending a conference.*
*He **crossed paths** with her when he was on business in New York.*

---

to meet (someone) by chance
*I hadn't seen her in months, but I **ran into** her at the trade show last week.*

---

to have a lot of work to do in order to accomplish something
*If he wants to finish this project before the trade show, he **has** his **work cut out for** him.*

---

to prepare oneself to accomplish something; to get organized
*We need to **get** our **act together** if we're going to finish this by Friday.*

on occasion

---

on the dot

---

back to the drawing board

---

third degree

---

drop by

sometimes
On occasion, I like to work from home.

---

at that exact time
We are meeting at 6:00 p.m. ***on the dot.***

---

to start from the beginning
Our permit was not approved, so we need to go ***back to the drawing board.***

---

intense interrogation
My boss gave me the ***third degree*** *about the unexplained expenses.*

---

to make a short, usually unannounced, visit
She ***dropped by*** *for a few minutes last night.*

drop in on someone

---

have one's **hands full**

---

go wrong

---

err on the side of caution

---

rest on one's **laurels**

to make a short, usually unannounced, visit (to a person)
*Before catching our flight home, we decided to **drop in on** one of our former clients.*

to be very busy; to have a lot to do
*He has **had** his **hands full** lately, so he probably won't be able to help you.*

to cause a failure; to go amiss
*The experiment failed, but scientists still aren't sure what could have **gone wrong**.*

to choose the safer alternative
*Until we have the due date confirmed, let's **err on the side of caution** and plan to complete the project by the end of July.*

to be satisfied with one's past accomplishments rather than attempting anything new
*Since her highly praised first novel came out, she has been **resting on** her **laurels** and hasn't written anything new.*
[a reference to the ancient Greek tradition of crowning a person with a wreath of laurels, or bay leaves, to honor a great accomplishment]

take one's **time**

---

tighten one's **belt**

---

touch on a subject

---

see eye to eye

---

have a say

to proceed slowly; to avoid rushing
*I'm **taking** my **time** on the proposal, since it isn't due until December.*

---

to take extreme measures in order to economize; to cut back
*Our funding has been cut, so we are going to have to **tighten** our **belts** and reduce the budget.*
[a reference to losing weight from eating less, which might cause someone to need a smaller belt]

---

to address (a topic) briefly
*Before we discuss Jack's role in the project, we should **touch on** our initial goals.*

---

to have similar opinions; to understand each other
*They have almost nothing in common, but when it comes to results they **see eye to eye**.*

---

to have a degree of influence or power
*It is important for employees to **have a say** in decisions about their office parties.*
*In a democracy, citizens **have a voice** in their government.*

cherry-pick

---

do someone **good**

---

narrow down

---

draw a blank

---

do one's **best**

to take only the most desirable items available from among a selection
*He sells the most cars because he **cherry-picks** the most promising customers, leaving the rest of us with the reluctant ones.*

to have a beneficial effect on (someone)
*She has seemed very stressed out lately; a vacation will **do** her **good**.*

to reduce the number of options in (a selection)
*They started with a pool of twenty applicants, but they were able to **narrow** it **down** to three finalists.*

to be unable to remember or respond
*I prepared thoroughly for the presentation, but when I stood up in front of the group, I **drew a blank**.*

to try as hard as possible
*He didn't get the job, but he **did** his **best**, and that is what really matters.*

pull the plug

---

pull someone's leg

---

six feet under

---

mom-and-pop

---

throw down the gauntlet

to end something
*The vice president **pulled the plug** on the project, citing unexpected expenditures.*

---

to joke or trick someone
*I really thought she had been fired, but she was just **pulling** my **leg**.*

---

deceased; dead
*Many of his colleagues were rude to him, and now that he is **six feet under**, many of them regret their behavior.*
[referring to the depth at which people are buried]

---

small, family-run business
*My favorite restaurant is a **mom-and-pop** place down the road.*

---

to issue a challenge
*Team A **threw down the gauntlet** to Team B, betting that they could sell more widgets in the next three months.*
[A gauntlet is a type of armored glove, which would traditionally be thrown down by a medieval knight in a challenge to an opponent. To accept the challenge, the opponent would pick up the glove; hence, to **take up the gauntlet** means "to accept a challenge."]

throw in the towel

---

throw someone **under the bus**

---

fill someone **in**

---

fill in for someone

---

take someone's **place**

to accept defeat; to surrender
*We struggled for many years with our business, but we finally **threw in the towel** after realizing we needed to make major renovations.*

to put the blame on someone else
*She claimed not to know anything about the scandal and **threw** her assistant **under the bus**.*

to inform (someone) fully; to give (someone) the details
*Lisa missed the meeting that included the budget proposal, so someone will have to **fill** her **in**.*

to replace or substitute for
*I usually work on weekdays only, but I'm **filling in for** Petros on Saturday.*

to replace or substitute for (someone)
*The lead presenter got sick, so I **took** his **place**.*

come to grips with something

---

stay out of a dispute

---

wear thin

---

speak out on a controversial issue

---

think up

to become capable of dealing with or understanding
*Many companies still haven't **come to grips with** the new regulations.*

---

to avoid getting involved in
*They were clearly having a dispute, but I **stayed out of** it and walked the other way.*

---

to become less effective due to overuse
*You claim to have run out of gas at least once a week, so that excuse is **wearing thin**.*

---

to express one's opinions openly
*It was nice to hear a politician **speak out** about the problems facing farmers today.*

---

to invent; to make up
*Our office manager is always **thinking up** new ways to welcome new hires.*

take advantage of someone or something

carry out orders

meet someone **halfway**

meet one's **match**

keep a low profile

1. to exploit (someone)
2. to utilize or avail oneself of (something)
*1. They had no real interest in being her friends; they were only **taking advantage of** her.*
*2.He is trying to **take advantage of** the many cultural experiences the city has to offer.*

---

to obey; to put into action
*She **carried out** your instructions perfectly; everything is exactly the way you wanted it.*

---

to compromise with (someone)
*We made several good offers, but he stubbornly stuck to his original quote and refused to **meet** us **halfway**.*

---

to find one's equal
*Liz is our top sales member, but she may have **met** her **match** in the new guy.*

---

to avoid getting attention or publicity
*After her embarrassing behavior at the last company party, she **kept a low profile** at this one.*

piece of cake

slap on the wrist

taste of your own medicine

a picture is worth a thousand words

get a message across

something that is easy
*Anand had prepared for months, so the TOEIC exam was a **piece of cake** for him.*

---

minor punishment
*Despite the fact that he had lost three top clients, the CEO's son received only a **slap on the wrist**.*

---

treatment similar to how you have been treating people
*One day someone will treat you poorly, and you will get a **taste of your own medicine**.*

---

you can learn more from a single picture than from many words
*She tried to describe the layout of the new office, but realized that **a picture is worth a thousand words**.*

---

to express
*The president's latest speech really **got across** his concern about the need for increasing employee tenure.*

get away with something

---

think on one's **feet**

---

wash one's **hands of**

---

settle for

---

cast doubt on something

to manage to escape the consequences of (an action)
*I can't believe she **got away with** submitting her expense report two months late.*

---

to react quickly and effectively without prior preparation
*He had to **think on** his **feet** when he was unexpectedly asked to lead the discussion.*

---

to claim to no longer be responsible for or involved with (something); to dissociate oneself from
*She **washed** her **hands of** that company when she discovered their questionable hiring practices.*

---

to accept less than desired or expected
*He had dreamed of becoming president of the United States, but he **settled for** being vice president of a large company.*

---

to make (something) appear doubtful or dubious
*The photos from the event **cast doubt on** her story.*

make a point of doing something

make do

make sure

make sense

keep an eye on something

to make a deliberate effort to do something
*I **make a point of** sharing my progress with the team on a weekly basis.*

---

to manage without something important; to get by
*Because the company was struggling financially, the employees had to **make do** without a holiday party.*

---

to be certain; to confirm
*Before leaving the house, he **made sure** he had his keys to the office.*

---

to be reasonable or logical
*Her theory **makes sense**.*

---

to watch; to monitor
*I asked Lindsey to **keep an eye on** the copy machine while I answered the phone.*

get over something

---

take someone's **word for it**

---

take a break

---

draw the line

---

think better of

to recover from; to bounce back from
*The team needs to **get over** today's loss and start preparing for the next client.*

---

to believe someone without additional evidence
*He says that he didn't take the money, and I'm **taking** his **word for it**.*

---

to take a rest; to stop an activity temporarily
*She worked on coding for hours at a time without **taking a break**.*

---

to set a limit about how far one is willing to go
*I'm willing to commute for a great job, but I **draw the line** at two hours round-trip.*

---

to decide against (doing something) after thinking about it more; to reconsider
*He had wanted to quit his job before finding another one, but he **thought better of it**.*

at the drop of a hat

---

an arm and a leg

---

bend over backward

---

cross your fingers

---

think something **over**

in a moment
*If she ever called, he would come to her side **at the drop of a hat**.*

---

a large amount (typically in reference to price)
*A flight to Europe used to be inexpensive, but now it costs **an arm and a leg**.*

---

to be overly accommodating, to do a large amount for someone
*Whenever she needed anything, he would **bend over backwards** for her.*

---

a gesture made for good luck
*I am going in for a big job interview today, so **cross your fingers** for me!*

---

to consider (something) carefully
*I probably won't accept the job offer, but I am still **thinking** it **over**.*

think twice

get rid of something

get the best of someone

get to the bottom of a mystery

get underway

to consider carefully before making a decision
*If I were you, I would **think twice** about responding to that job ad.*

to discard or eliminate
*We **got rid of** all the food in the break room refrigerator that was past its due date.*

to defeat or outwit
*He tried to stay awake for the phone call from the team in India, but his fatigue **got the best of** him and he fell asleep before 11:00.*

to uncover the truth about
*We reported the strange sounds coming from the elevator and the repairman promised to **get to the bottom of** it.*

to begin; to start
*Our national business meeting **gets underway** on Monday.*

mince words

jump on the bandwagon

make good on a promise

make off with

stand for something

to avoid directly saying something which might upset or offend
*Tell me what you really thought of my presentation and don't **mince words**.*

---

to take up an activity or idea that is suddenly very popular
*The price of the stock rose quickly as many investors **jumped on the bandwagon** and bought shares.*

---

to follow through on
*The company **made good on** its pledge to donate new computers to the school.*

---

to take or steal (something); to abscond with
*The executive vice president was caught trying to **make off with** several computers.*

---

1. to support or advocate (a belief or principle)
2. to be an abbreviation of
1. *His memorial should express the ideals he **stood for** all his life: freedom and equality.*
2. *CEO **stands for** chief executive officer.*

stand up for someone

stand out

wind down

wind up somewhere

keep at something

to defend; to advocate for
*Her boss **stood up for** her when she was almost fired for the error.*

---

to be conspicuous; to attract attention
*Of all of our trainees, he **stands out** as the most promising.*

---

1. to slow down; to draw to a close
2. to relax (said of a person)
*1. This is the time of the season when our business begins to **wind down**.*
*2. After five days of back-to-back meetings, I definitely need to **wind down** this weekend.*

---

to find oneself in a place or situation; to arrive or end up
*I was as surprised as anyone when I **wound up** working in our Tennessee office.*

---

to continue to do; to persist or persevere with
*She had trouble at first, but she **kept at** it and is now one of the top analysts in the company.*

hit the books

---

hit the hay

---

hit the nail on the head

---

eighth wonder

---

keep information **from** someone

to study
*I didn't study my TOEIC vocabulary over spring break; now it is time to **hit the books**.*

---

to go to sleep
*The company meeting is at 7:00 a.m., so I am going to **hit the hay** early tonight.*

---

to understand something precisely
*You just **hit the nail on the head**; I knew you would understand.*

---

something remarkable
*I don't understand how their science experiment ever worked, it is the **eighth wonder** of the world.*
[in reference to the seven wonders of the world]

---

to hide (something) from someone; to keep (something) secret from someone
*Winston **kept** the news of the impending layoffs **from** his employees.*

keep from doing something

keep up with someone or something

lend a hand

jump to conclusions

sit around

to stop from doing something; to refrain from or avoid
*It took all our persuasive skills to **keep** her **from** quitting immediately.*

---

1. to travel at the same speed as; to stay abreast of
2. to stay informed about
*1. The presentation was very advanced, and he couldn't **keep up with** everyone.*
*2. I try to **keep up with** the latest advances in computer science.*

---

to help
*I was proud that my company **lent a hand** to the effort to rebuild after the earthquake.*
*Could you please **give** me **a hand** with this heavy box?*

---

to form an opinion about something quickly without examining all of the facts
*A good doctor looks at all of a patient's symptoms carefully before making a diagnosis, rather than just **jumping to conclusions**.*

---

to lounge or be idle; to hang around
*She used to exercise a lot, but now she just **sits around** working on her new app.*

sit through

sit tight

get on with an activity

take a piece of information **into account**

show up

to stay to the end of (an event or performance)
*The demo fair was too long, and it was difficult to **sit through** for three hours.*

---

to wait patiently
*Could you just **sit tight** for a little bit longer? I'm almost ready to leave.*

---

to continue
*We need to stop wasting time and **get on with** reviewing our notes.*

---

to consider; to give attention to
*The theory was flawed because it didn't **take into account** the importance of environmental factors.*

---

to arrive
*He didn't **show up** at work until after 11:00 am.*

show someone **up**

split hairs

go without saying

take something **in stride**

wipe something **out**

to embarrass or outperform (someone)
She **showed up** the team leader by appearing more prepared and knowledgeable in the presentation.

to make small, unimportant distinctions
They still haven't agreed on the final wording of the contract, but they are just **splitting hairs** at this point; all of the important issues have been decided.

to be obvious or self-evident
It **goes without saying** that you should wear professional clothes to a job interview.

to deal with (something difficult) in a calm way, so that it does not cause disruptions
The players **took** the insults of the opposing team **in stride** and focused on winning the company softball game.

to destroy (something) completely
The unexpected expenses **wiped out** any chance of profitability.

off the hook

off the record

on the fence

on the same page

save one's breath

to get away with something, to suffer no punishment
*The cop let him **off the hook** with a warning.*

---

something that is not written down
*Everything she told me, she told me **off the record**.*

---

not able to decide
*I really want to go to Miami for the publishing conference, but I am **on the fence** because it is very expensive.*

---

to be in understanding
*When he told me his vision for the project, I knew we were **on the same page**.*

---

to refrain from saying something that is useless or unnecessary
*She won't change her mind no matter what you say, so **save** your **breath**.*

save face

fill out a form

bide one's **time**

keep her **on** her **toes**

keep track of

to preserve one's dignity or honor; to avoid embarrassment
*He **saved face** by resigning from his job before he could be fired.*

---

to complete (a form)
*She has **filled out** the last three job applications.*

---

to wait patiently
*Although he didn't get the promotion, he is **biding** his **time** until the next opportunity.*

---

to force (someone) to stay alert
*Our supervisor **keeps** us **on** our **toes** by asking questions throughout the meeting.*

---

to keep a record of; to stay informed about
*Samantha **kept track of** her expenses so that she could be reimbursed.*

slip someone's **mind**

pave the way

take it easy

ring a bell

put the rumors **to rest**

to be forgotten by someone
*I was supposed to call the client back, but it completely **slipped** my **mind**.*

---

to make future accomplishments possible; to prepare the way
*When she was promoted to president, she realized she was **paving the way** for other women in the company.*
[*Way* is an old-fashioned word for road; *paving* a road makes it easier and faster to travel on.]

---

to relax; to be idle
*Last summer I worked 60 hours a week, but this year I am **taking it easy**.*

---

to bring back a memory; to sound familiar
*I don't recognize his face, but his voice **rings a bell**.*

---

to put a stop to; to end; to quell
*If you are afraid of flying, the new technology in these planes should **put** your fears **to rest**.*

pin down the details

field questions

count as

count on

keep something **at bay**

to define firmly; to figure out
*We know the conference will be held in Palm Springs, but we haven't **pinned down** a date yet.*

to answer questions from a group of people
*After her speech, she **fielded questions** from the audience.*

to be considered; to qualify as
*At many U.S. companies, Independence Day **counts as** a paid holiday.*

to rely on; to depend on
*We need to fly out to California because Rick is **counting on** us for help with the new client.*

to make (something) stay away; to ward off
*The new software is designed to **keep** viruses **at bay**.*

start from scratch

the nines

let on

icing on the cake

figure out

start from the beginning
*The leadership team changed its mind, so Eva had to **start** the study **from scratch**.*

___

to perfection
*When he went to the company holiday party, he was dressed to **the nines**.*

___

to admit or acknowledge
*I think she knows more than she is willing to **let on**.*

___

an additional benefit
*He loves the job offer and was extremely excited to take it; the extra vacation time was just **icing on the cake**.*

___

to determine or conclude
*The engineer **figured out** that the problems were being caused by a faulty part.*

cut back on something

---

cut off

---

cut to the chase

---

come around

---

come down to

to use or do less of (something)
*Lucas needs to **cut back on** his hours, or he'll go into overtime.*

---

1. to interrupt
2. to stop or discontinue
*1. She rudely **cut** him **off** in the middle of his story.*
*2. Her system access was **cut off** on her last day.*

---

to get directly to the point
*Jack started describing all of the different features, but we were in a hurry, so we asked him to **cut to the chase**.*

---

to agree to something eventually
*My husband doesn't like how much I have to travel in my new job, but I'm sure he'll **come around**.*

---

to have as an essential point; to be dependent upon
*Whether or not we hire her for this position **comes down to** her experience.*

come along

---

bear fruit

---

take its toll

---

put off an activity

---

pass up an opportunity

1. to accompany
2. to progress
1. He invited his wife to **come along** on his business trip.
2. There were a lot of construction problems at first, but the new house is finally **coming along**.

---

to produce results; to be successful
*After twenty years of research, our effort to cure the disease is finally **bearing fruit**.*

---

to have a negative effect
*The fast turnaround **took its toll** on the team, but we completed it in time.*

---

to postpone
*He **put off** the ancement until Monday.*

---

to decline; to fail to take advantage of
*She **passed up** a job offer at a prestigious law firm because she wanted to make a difference in the public sector.*

put one's **finger on** a piece of information

---

fall apart at the seams

---

fall short

---

fall into place

---

fall out with someone

to identify; to pinpoint
*There must be something missing, but I can't **put** my **finger on** what it is.*

---

doing very poorly, extremely unwell
*We are worried about him; ever since he was laid off, he has been **falling apart at the seams**.*

---

to fail to meet expectations
*Our profits for last year **fell short** of our projections.*

---

to turn out as hoped for
*We were afraid that we would never finish planning our speech, but everything seems to be **falling into place**.*

---

to have a serious disagreement
*They **fell out with** each other years ago over who would run the family business.*
Also as a noun: to have a **falling out** with someone.

turn a blind eye to a problem

cry wolf

gut feeling

actions speak louder than words

take note of something

to ignore; to overlook
*The manager accused the employees of **turning a blind eye** to the issues with theft.*

---

to claim something is happening when it isn't
*She warned the new hire not to label all her email as urgent, or she would become known as someone who **cried wolf**.*

---

the feeling of your intuition
*I had a **gut feeling** something was wrong, so I gave him a call.*

---

what you do is more important than what you say
*She is always saying how much she cares, but then she is never around. She doesn't realize that her **actions speak louder than** her **words**.*

---

to notice; to observe
*I looked around and **took note of** the obvious hierarchy among the employees.*

muddle through

bring someone **up to date**

put something **on hold**

rule out a possibility

play down an achievement

to find a way in spite of difficulty or disorganization; to manage
*I didn't know anything about how to manage a project, but I **muddled through**.*

---

to give (someone) the latest information
*After my two-week vacation, I asked one of my coworkers to **bring** me **up to date**.*

---

to stop (something) temporarily; to suspend
*We are **putting** the renovation **on hold** until next summer.*

---

to exclude (something) as a possible option or explanation
*We haven't **ruled out** opening a new location, but it's still too early to decide.*

---

to minimize the importance of
*Jenna always **played down** how skilled she was with the program.*
The opposite is *to **play up***: "to exaggerate."

play it safe

---

play with fire

---

keep something **in mind**

---

bargain for

---

deal with a situation

to avoid taking risks
*They **played it safe** and allowed two hours for the drive to the airport.*

---

to do something dangerous or risky
*We warned the diplomat that she was **playing with fire** by getting involved in local politics.*

---

to remember and account for (something)
*When writing a speech, it is important to **keep in mind** who your audience is.*

---

to expect or be prepared for
*We received hundreds more applicants than we had **bargained for** initially.*

---

to handle or control
*They are finding new ways of **dealing with** the rising import costs.*

take over an organization

run out of something

take on someone or something

beat around the bush

put down roots

to take control of
*He is difficult to work with because he usually tries to **take over** the most interesting projects.*

---

to use up (a supply of something)
*My phone always **runs out of** battery life by 4:00 p.m.*

---

1. to hire (an employee)
2. to confront; to fight against
1. *They decided to **take** her **on** as a research assistant.*
2. *The environmental group is **taking on** a big corporation it accuses of polluting the lake.*

---

to avoid talking directly about something
*The community meeting was frustrating, because the mayor kept **beating around the bush** instead of addressing the important issues facing our community.*

---

to settle down; to establish a permanent residence
*After years of traveling, he is finally **putting down roots** by buying a house in his hometown.*

great minds think alike

---

the ball is in your court

---

third time's a charm

---

tie the knot

---

put up with something unpleasant

intelligent people think the same way
After I told her my plan, she told me that it was exactly what she had been planning; I guess **great minds think alike**.

---

it is your decision
Now that you have all information, **the ball is in your court**.

---

you are likely to succeed on the third try
I missed the bus two days in a row; hopefully the **third time's a charm**.

---

to get married
They have been dating for ten years and are ready to **tie the knot**.

---

to endure or tolerate
Rather than addressing their tardiness, he **puts up with** *their behavior*.

take part

---

take sides

---

talk someone **into** doing something

---

put the cart before the horse

---

make up one's **mind**

to participate
*Both divisions **took part** in the decision.*

to align oneself with one of the sides in a dispute
*Managers should avoid **taking sides**.*

to convince (someone) to do something
*She didn't want to join the firm, but they **talked** her **into** it.*

to do things in the wrong order
*Critics say that buying furniture for the new office building before the architect has been chosen is **putting the cart before the horse**.*

to decide; to make a decision
*He received two different job offers, so now he is trying to **make up** his **mind** about which one to accept.*

pay the price for something

take a stab at doing something

part with something

take something **with a grain of salt**

mud on one's **face**

to bear the consequences of a mistake or misdeed
*We all had to **pay the price** for missing the deadline and work on Saturday.*

---

to try; to make an attempt
*They asked her to **take a stab at** creating a web page.*

---

to give (something) up
*Even when he was promoted, he refused to **part with** his office chair.*

---

to be skeptical about (something)
*Since she has strong views on this subject, you should **take** her report **with a grain of salt**.*

---

to be embarrassed
*When the newspaper published the article about his company's financial problems, the executive had **mud on** his **face**.*

wear many hats

worth one's **salt**

off guard

on an even keel

above board

to fill many roles
*As a CEO, wife, and mother, she **wears many hats** on a daily basis.*

---

competent at one's profession
*Any manager **worth** his **salt** would have taught you how to effectively carry out a project.*

---

unprepared
*She did well for most of the interview, but she was caught **off guard** by the last question.*

---

steady and balanced; moving calmly forward
*The local economy went through some difficult times when the factory closed, but it has been **on an even keel** for many years.*
Also **even-keeled**: *He has an **even-keeled** personality.*
[A *keel* is a structure on the bottom of a boat that keeps it stable.]

---

conducted lawfully and openly; legitimate; honest
*The deal sounded suspicious, but my lawyer assured me that it was completely **above board**.*

best of both worlds

---

make a long story short

---

wine and dine

---

judge a book by its cover

---

blue-collar

get the positive aspects of two things at once
*I just got a new job offer to write a book from home, so I will be doing what I love and spending time with my family. It is truly the **best of both worlds**.*

---

to shorten a story to get to the point
*To **make a long story short**, she no longer works for the company.*

---

to impress someone, usually with a fancy meal and drinks
*Whenever new clients came to town, he did his best to **wine and dine** them.*

---

to judge by appearance instead of merit
*She didn't look like a nice person, but when I talked to her I was pleasantly surprised. It just goes to show that you should never **judge a book by its cover**.*

---

involving or denoting physical labor
*During the summer, he does various **blue-collar** jobs like construction work and house painting.*

white-collar

---

run of the mill

---

on the tip of one's **tongue**

---

beside the point

---

to the point

denoting administrative or clerical work that does not involve physical labor
*The Internet boom has created a lot of office jobs for **white-collar** workers.*

---

unexceptional; ordinary
*Despite all of the praise she has gotten lately, I think she is really just a **run-of-the-mill** manager.*

---

on the verge of being remembered
*I can't quite recall his name, but it's **on the tip of** my **tongue**.*

---

irrelevant; unimportant
*The real issue in the renovation is that we need more space; the color of the carpet is **beside the point**.*

---

directly related to the topic at hand; relevant
*After many revisions, her report was succinct and **to the point**.*

at a loss for words

---

neither here nor there

---

down to earth

---

down and out

---

in check

unable to think of anything to say; speechless
*When they offered him the role, he was **at a loss for words**.*

---

unimportant or irrelevant
*We accept anyone who can play chess; your age is **neither here nor there**.*

---

reasonable and practical; realistic
*She seems remarkably **down to earth** for the CFO of such a successful company.*

---

very poor; destitute
*He was a **down-and-out** alcoholic a decade ago, but today he owns his own business and has been sober for eight years.*

---

under control
*Now that our budget is tighter, we will have to keep our spending **in check**.*

beside oneself

full-fledged

no-win situation

win-win situation

in charge of

extremely agitated or upset; distraught
*After being stuck in traffic for two hours and missing the entire meeting, he was **beside himself** with worry.*

---

complete; mature; fully developed
*Her hobby of baking cookies has become a **full-fledged** business, with stores all over the city.*

---

having no possibility of a positive outcome
*It was a **no-win** situation: we either had to pay the fine or pay a lawyer to fight it.*

---

denoting a situation in which both parties benefit
*He will gain professional experience and you will receive a web page at a discount: it's a **win-win** arrangement.*

---

responsible for; in control of
*You will be **in charge of** refreshments for our next meeting.*

when it rains, it pours

when pigs fly

your guess is as good as mine

break a leg

on the right track

when one good/bad thing happens, many good/bad things happen
*I woke up late, spilled coffee down the front of my shirt, and hit traffic on the way to work; **when it rains, it pours***.

---

unlikely to happen
*She will be on time for training **when pigs fly***.

I'm not any more certain than you are
*I think he said we should be there at 4 p.m., but **your guess is as good as mine***.

---

good luck
***Break a leg** in your presentation this afternoon!*

---

following a course that is likely to be successful
*I don't know the answer yet, but I think I am **on the right track***.

on the wrong track

---

on the fence

---

on the horizon

---

red-handed

---

is short for

following a course that is likely to fail
*She hasn't been making progress with her research and seems to be **on the wrong track**.*

---

undecided; unable to make up one's mind
*He is still **on the fence** about which candidate to vote for.*

---

coming up in the near future
*We aren't very busy at the moment, but we have some major projects **on the horizon**.*

---

in the act of committing a crime
*They caught the thief **red-handed** with the stolen cash in her pockets.*

---

used as an abbreviation or shortened form of
*Did you know that the word "info" **is short for** "information"?*
Also **for short**: *Theodore is called Ted **for short**.*

wrapped up in something

up in the air

in short supply

low-key

feeling up to something

preoccupied with; completely absorbed in
*He was so **wrapped up in** working on his laptop that he didn't hear me walk in.*

---

unresolved; not yet settled
*We want to hold the company party there, but our plans are still **up in the air**.*

---

scarce; insufficiently available; running out
*We have plenty of paper left, but ink cartridges are **in short supply**.*

---

relaxed; laid-back; restrained
*We are having a retirement party for Walter. It will be very small and **low-key,** with just a few of us present.*

---

ready for or able to do something
*I know you've been ill. Are you **feeling up to** leading the meeting?*

in the pipeline

on the same page

in touch with someone

at a premium

in the wings

on the way; being developed
*She published two books last year, and she already has another one **in the pipeline**.*

---

in complete agreement
*They had some arguments about the renovation in the beginning, but now they are **on the same page**.*

---

in contact with; in communication with
*We used to be close friends, but I haven't kept **in touch with** him for several years now.*
*I really hope that I will keep **in touch with** my work friends after I move.*

---

particularly valuable; especially in demand
*In today's job market, computer skills are **at a premium**.*

---

ready to act or be used at any time
*There were many people waiting **in the wings** to take over when she retired.*
[a reference to the *wings* of a theater, where actors wait to go on stage]

let the cat out of the bag

once in a blue moon

a penny for your thoughts

cut corners

in the works

to tell a secret
*The retirement party was supposed to be a surprise, but his manager accidentally **let the cat out of the bag**.*

---

rarely
*She only calls if she needs something, which only happens **once in a blue moon**.*

---

a way to ask someone what they are thinking
*You have been awfully quiet; **a penny for your thoughts**?*

---

take shortcuts
*In order to save money, he often **cuts corners**, which will likely cost him more money in the long run.*

---

being planned or produced; in process
*A second draft of the proposal is **in the works**.*

in line with something

---

at the mercy of

---

on top of a task

---

time-honored

---

on the table

in accordance with; consistent with
*The skills needed for this job are **in line with** her previous roles.*

---

completely under the control of; powerless against; totally dependent upon
*This project is truly **at the mercy of** the budget.*

---

doing everything necessary to accomplish (something); in control of
*I offered to help with the decorations for the office party, but Danielle said she was **on top of** it.*

---

traditional; long-standing
*Closing early on December 24th is a **time-honored** custom in the United States.*

---

up for discussion; possible as an option
*We haven't made a final decision yet, so all of the proposals are still **on the table**.*

of few words

---

out of the question

---

worse for wear

---

thin-skinned

---

light years ahead

not talkative; reticent
*Melanie is a woman **of few words**, but when she says something it is usually very insightful.*

---

impossible; inconceivable; not worth considering
*Because of the recent snowstorm, it was **out of the question** to expect all the employees to get to the office.*

---

showing signs of age or use
*The couch in the lobby is eight years old and a bit **worse for wear**.*

---

extremely sensitive; easily upset
*When employees are too **thin-skinned**, it can be difficult to give them feedback on their work.*
The opposite is **thick-skinned**.

---

far ahead; far more advanced
*Their science laboratories are **light years ahead** of the facilities at our university.*

out of hand

---

grass-roots

---

fine tuning

---

easy as pie

---

one in a million

unmanageable; out of control
*The absenteeism at this branch is getting **out of hand**.*

---

based on the efforts of ordinary people
*Our new city council member didn't get a lot of support from powerful politicians, although he had a strong **grass-roots** campaign.*

---

minor adjustments needed to perfect something
*The presentation is almost done, but it still needs a bit of **fine tuning**.*
Also as a verb: *We need to **fine-tune** our performance.*

---

very simple
*Since she had studied so hard, she thought the TOEIC exam was **easy as pie**.*

---

unique; unusual
*The company knew they'd found **one in a million** when they hired him for the job.*

wet behind the ears

green

foregone conclusion

odds and ends

level playing field

new; untested
*Ed doesn't know yet how his company's e-mail system works, because he's only been here one day and is still **wet behind the ears**.*

---

inexperienced; new
*Her first interview with the applicant went too long, because she was still **green** and didn't know which questions to ask.*

---

an obvious outcome; a result which can be predicted in advance
*Because of the attorney's superior defense, it was a **foregone conclusion** that the jury would acquit.*

---

an assortment of random things
*His desk was covered with **odds and ends**, so it was impossible to find anything.*

---

fairness; equality
*Public schools are intended to create a **level playing field** in education.*

mixed emotions

powers that be

light at the end of the tunnel

white elephant

lame duck

positive and negative feelings felt at the same time
*She has **mixed emotions** about accepting the job offer; it will pay well, but she doesn't really want to relocate.*

the people who have authority
*No changes can be made without approval from the **powers that be**.*

hope that a time of difficulty will end
*The company struggled for years to be profitable, and there is finally **light at the end of the tunnel**.*

a possession that is useless or unwanted, and difficult to get rid of
*The painting in the lobby is valuable, but no one likes looking at a picture of a slaughterhouse, so it's really a **white elephant**.*

a person who is currently in a position of authority, but whose successor has already been chosen
*When a sitting U.S. president loses the election for a second term in November, he becomes a **lame duck** until the new president is inaugurated the following January.*

second wind

last minute

last resort

last straw

white lie

a new burst of energy or strength to continue a difficult effort
*The sales team got its **second wind** after a long day of presentations.*
[originally used to describe the sudden ability to breathe more easily that some people feel after exercising for a long time]

---

the latest possible time
*She always leaves her expense reports until the **last minute**.*
Also as an adjective: ***last-minute** Christmas shopping.*

---

the final option remaining when everything else has failed
*Closing the branch in Ohio is the **last resort** to cut costs.*

---

the last of a series of problems or annoyances, which causes someone to finally give up
*We have put up with a leaky roof, broken elevator, and heating problems in the factory, but the breakdown of the air-conditioning system was the **last straw**.*

---

a lie considered to be harmless, often told out of politeness
*I told him he did well on the presentation, but it was a **white lie**, as he did really poorly.*

salt of the earth

---

yellow journalism

---

the lesser of two evils

---

red tape

---

small talk

a person who is decent, honest, kind, and unpretentious
*The owners of the company are very nice people, the **salt of the earth**.*
Often used as an adjective: ***salt-of-the-earth*** *people*.

---

journalism that is sensationalist and biased
*That newspaper will print anything to sell papers—it's all gossip and **yellow journalism**.*

---

an option which is bad, but still better than the alternative
*I wasn't impressed with either of the candidates, but I voted for **the lesser of two evils**.*

---

excessive regulations and bureaucracy
*We had to deal with a lot of **red tape** to get the proper visa to travel here.*
[From the red-colored tape or ribbon that was once used to tie together bundles of legal documents]

---

polite conversation on unimportant topics; chat
*She made **small talk** with all of the guests at the company party.*

tip of the iceberg

---

no time to lose

---

double-edged sword

---

sticking point

---

zero tolerance

a small but easily recognized part of a much larger problem or issue
*The corruption scandals reported in the news are only the **tip of the iceberg**.*
[a reference to the fact that most of an iceberg is hidden underneath the water—only the tip is visible]

there is no extra time; action must be taken right away
*There is **no time to lose**, so let's get to work.*

something that has the potential both to help and to hurt
*His talent is a **double-edged sword**: it brings him success, but it has also limited his options.*

a controversial issue that is an obstacle to making an agreement
*They are close to signing a contract, but the number of vacation days is still a **sticking point**.*

a policy of punishing even minor offenses
*The office has instituted a policy of **zero tolerance** for dress-code violations; last week, an employee was written up for forgetting to wear a tie.*
Also as an adjective: *a **zero-tolerance** approach to law enforcement.*

mint condition

---

upper hand

---

bad blood

---

game plan

---

cutting edge

in excellent condition, as if new
*These antique toys are very valuable because they are still in **mint condition**.*
Also as an adjective: *a **mint-condition** car.*
[in reference to *mint*, a place where coins are made]

---

the better position in a situation; the advantage
*When the competitor lost its president, we quickly gained the **upper hand**.*

---

hostility due to past events; ill will; antagonism; hatred
*There has been **bad blood** between them ever since the lawsuit ten years ago.*

---

a strategy
*What is your **game plan** for increasing profits?*

---

the forefront of progress within a field
*This scientist is doing projects on the **cutting edge** of physics research.*
Also used as an adjective: ***cutting-edge** technology.*

Achilles' heel

clean slate

gray area

face value

about face

the one weak spot of an otherwise strong person
*Though I am generally good in English, her first question found my **Achilles' heel**: my ignorance of spelling rules.*
[in reference to the character *Achilles* in Greek mythology, who could be injured only on his heel]

---

a fresh start, with any previous mistakes forgiven or forgotten
*He moved to a new city, where he could start over with a **clean slate**.*

---

an issue about which there is no clear answer, or where conventional standards don't seem to apply
*A lot of Internet businesses operate in a **gray area**, and no one is sure what laws should apply to them.*

---

1. the value printed on a ticket, note of currency, etc.
2. the apparent or superficial meaning of something
*1. We paid more than **face value** for the concert tickets.*
*2. If you take her last speech at **face value**, it sounds like she is planning radical changes.*

---

a complete reversal; a U-turn
*After ten years of supporting the same party, he did an **about face** and started voting for the opposition.*

what it takes

---

vicious cycle/circle

---

eleventh hour

---

bitter pill

---

uncharted waters

the qualities required to accomplish something
*Linda has **what it takes** to become a board member.*

---

a cycle of negative effects that build off of one another, resulting in a worsening situation; a downward spiral
*The company was stuck in a **vicious cycle** of not making money and needing to lay people off.*
*Because the shop didn't have enough inventory, customers didn't come to it; because there weren't enough customers, the shop couldn't afford more inventory. It was a **vicious circle**.*

---

the last possible moment
*They waited until the **eleventh hour** to make plans for their business trip, so they had trouble getting a hotel room.*
*Also as an adjective: an **eleventh-hour** effort to conclude the talks.*

---

an unpleasant fact that is difficult to accept
*It was a **bitter pill** to swallow that profits were down for the fifth month in a row.*

---

a new or unfamiliar situation
*Advances in biotechnology are taking scientists into **uncharted waters**, which require new ethical guidelines.*

rule of thumb

---

hard feelings

---

true colors

---

bells and whistles

---

salad days

a general or approximate guideline
*When cooking rice, a good **rule of thumb** is to use two parts water to one part rice.*

negative feelings of resentment or bitterness
*They are no longer in business together, but they are still friends, and there are no **hard feelings** about the end of their partnership.*

a person's real or authentic character
*She seems very calm and polite, but her angry outburst yesterday revealed her **true colors**.*

attractive but unnecessary extra features
*For a little more money, you can get the deluxe version of the car with all the **bells and whistles**.*

the days of one's youth, regarded either as a time of inexperience or as a peak or heyday
*We recalled the rash decisions of our **salad days**.*

labor of love

---

olive branch

---

big picture

---

ill-gotten gains

---

quantum leap

a project undertaken purely out of pleasure or interest
*The chef ran the business well; however, cooking was his **labor of love**.*

---

a gesture of peace
*After a hard-fought campaign, the winning politician offered her opponents an **olive branch** by inviting them to join her cabinet.*

---

the broad perspective on an issue; the overview
*The proposal should focus on the **big picture**; we don't want to get bogged down in the details.*

---

profits or benefits acquired unfairly or illegally
*Robin Hood is both a thief and a hero, because he shares his **ill-gotten gains** with the poor.*

---

a sudden and significant improvement or advance
*In the past decade, there has been a **quantum leap** in our scientific under-standing of human genetics.*
[from physics, where a *quantum leap* is the abrupt shift of an electron within an atom from one energy state to another]

state of the art

---

recipe for disaster

---

hollow victory

Pyrrhic victory

---

ivory tower

the latest, most up-to-date technology
*His new stereo is the **state of the art** in audio equipment.*
Also as an adjective: ***state-of-the-art*** *technology.*

---

a plan or set of circumstances that is doomed to produce terrible results
*Assigning the two of them to work on a project together is a **recipe for disaster**.*

---

a victory that accomplishes or signifies nothing
*She won the race, but since all of the best competitors had dropped out, it was a **hollow victory**.*

---

a victory that comes at too high a cost, leaving the winner worse off
*Nuclear deterrence is based on the fact that to win a nuclear war would result in a **Pyrrhic victory**.*

---

a place that is insulated from the concerns of the real world
*To better understand the morale issues, the CEO should come out of his **ivory tower** and talk to employees.*

change of pace

---

bottom line

---

across the board

---

at odds with

---

off the cuff

a change from what is usual or ordinary
The marketing team decided to focus on a different social-media service for a ***change of pace***.

---

the most important consideration or conclusion; the main point
We talked about a lot of techniques for time management, but the ***bottom line*** *is that we just need to get more done.*
[from the use of *the bottom line* in accounting, where it refers to the final total of a balance sheet]

---

for all; in every category
The new budget makes cutbacks in government services ***across the board****, from highways to education.*

---

in contradiction to; in disagreement or conflicting with
Her account of events is ***at odds with*** *the story published in the newspaper.*

---

without any preparation
Everyone was impressed when he gave a fantastic speech ***off the cuff****.*

now and then

_____

hand in hand

_____

in the dark

_____

down the road

_____

ahead of time

occasionally
*The staff goes out for a drink together **now and then**.*

---

1. holding hands
2. in close association; jointly
1. *Couples walked down the street **hand in hand**.*
2. *Low unemployment often goes **hand in hand** with inflation.*

---

without important information; uninformed
*She was upset that they had kept her **in the dark** about their plan to sell the company.*

---

in the future
*This may seem like a risky investment now, but I am confident that it will pay off **down the road**.*

---

in advance; beforehand
*She practiced an acceptance speech **ahead of time** just in case she won the prize.*

at stake

---

in the wake of

---

through thick and thin

---

to speak of

---

without a doubt

at risk; in question
*Given the financial challenges of our department, we have a lot **at stake** with this account.*

as a consequence of; in the aftermath of
***In the wake of** the recent earthquake, we decided to redesign the building for stability.*

through good times and bad times; in all circumstances
*The boss urged everyone to stay with the company **through thick and thin**.*

worth mentioning
*The company didn't make any profit **to speak of** in the first year.*

certainly; absolutely; unquestionably
*It was **without a doubt** the worst presentation I have ever seen.*

on top of

---

out of the blue

---

as far as someone **knows**

---

on one's **mind**

---

behind closed doors

in addition to; besides
On top of *all of his other accomplishments, he is now president of the company.*

---

without any warning; unexpectedly; out of nowhere
*I hadn't seen her in months, but she called me **out of the blue** last week and invited me to dinner.*

---

based on the information (a person) has; to the best of (a person's) knowledge
*He isn't here yet, but **as far as** I **know** he is still planning to lead the meeting.*

---

in one's thoughts; preoccupying one
*I have a lot **on** my **mind** right now.*
*That incident has been **on** her **mind** lately.*

---

in secret; out of public view
*The company eventually signed the contract, but we may never know what bargains were made **behind closed doors** to make it happen.*

on behalf of someone

---

be that as it may

---

under the table

---

firsthand

---

on and off/off and on

as a representative of someone; in the interest of someone
*He wrote a letter **on behalf of** his mother, asking the company to give her a refund.*

---

nevertheless
*Some say that printed books are becoming obsolete; **be that as it may**, publishing remains a dynamic and prosperous business.*

---

without proper permission or disclosure; illegally
*She was getting paid **under the table** to avoid taxes.*

---

personally; directly; in person
*I had heard that the new factory was impressive, but I didn't appreciate its immensity until I saw it **firsthand**.*

---

with interruptions; intermittently
*It rained **on and off** all night, but never for very long.*
*The internet connection has been **off and on** all week.*

in a nutshell

---

down the line

---

to a fault

---

word of mouth

---

behind someone's **back**

in a short summary; very briefly
*This summary covers the major points of the topic **in a nutshell**.*

in the future; eventually
*This may seem like a good policy now, but it could cause major problems **down the line**.*

excessively; so much that it causes problems
*He is careful **to a fault**; it takes him forever to finish anything.*

through informal conversation
*They didn't have enough money to advertise in the newspaper, but they got a lot of publicity by **word of mouth**.*
Also as an adjective: ***word-of-mouth*** advertising.

when someone is not around
*It is unfair to criticize her **behind** her **back**, when she can't defend himself.*

behind the scenes

---

all of a sudden

---

beyond a/the shadow of a doubt

---

in the balance

---

in over one's **head**

out of public view
*The agreement between the two leaders seemed spontaneous, but a lot of negotiations were conducted **behind the scenes** to make it happen.*
[a reference to theaters, where preparations take place behind the scenery, out of sight of the audience]

---

without any warning; instantly
*We were on a videoconference call when **all of a sudden** my screen froze.*

---

without any doubt at all; for certain
*We are certain, **beyond a shadow of a doubt**, that this is the right direction.*

---

at stake; at risk
*Looking for a job is very stressful; sometimes it feels like your entire future is **in the balance**.*

---

in a situation for which one is not qualified or prepared
*She got **in over** her **head** when she agreed to do all of the paperwork for the project.*

by the book

---

as far as someone **is concerned**

---

in no time

---

by virtue of

---

for the time being

according to the rules or directions; correctly
*There weren't any violations—he did everything **by the book**.*

---

in someone's opinion
*I thought it was a great review, but **as far as** she **is concerned** it was the worst she'd ever received.*

---

very quickly; right away
*The new network is almost done; it will be ready **in no time**.*

---

because of; on the basis of
*He got the job **by virtue of** his superior language skills.*

---

for now; at this time, but not necessarily in the future
*Let's keep this project a secret **for the time being**.*

by all means

---

by no means

---

as usual

---

back to/at square one

---

in view of

certainly; definitely
*If you go to the conference in New York City, **by all means**, visit the Empire State Building.*

---

absolutely not; not at all
*She is a talented writer but **by no means** the best in the department.*

---

as ordinarily or habitually happens; like always
*I planned to be on time today, but **as usual** I overslept.*

---

back to the point where one started, as if no progress had been made
*If this doesn't work, we can go **back to square one**.*
*Their first plan failed, so now they are **back at square one**.*

---

considering; taking into account
*His writing is especially impressive **in view of** the fact that English is not his first language.*

in the long run

---

by the way

---

for the most part

---

as yet

---

in light of

after a long time; in the end; eventually
*It may seem hard to save money for retirement now, but **in the long run** you will be very glad that you did.*

---

incidentally
*I read that book you lent me. **By the way,** did you know the author lives near here?*

---

in general; mostly
*Her results this year were good **for the most part**.*

---

up to the present time; as of now
*They will be hiring a new secretary, but **as yet** they have not done so.*

---

considering; because of; taking into account
*He was given a lighter punishment **in light of** the fact that this was the first time he had broken the rules.*

for good measure

---

against all/the odds

---

by hand

---

the looks of

---

on the spot

in addition; beyond what is needed
*My boss asked me for one proposal, but I did a second **for good measure**.*

---

despite it being very unlikely; incredibly, unexpectedly
***Against all odds**, we beat the competition and got the client.*
*She recovered from the operation and, **against the odds**, was able to walk again.*

---

without using a machine
*He prefers calculating **by hand** instead of using a calculator.*

---

based on the appearance of something; apparently
*From **the looks of** the orientation, there must be fewer new hires this quarter.*
*The bake sale is raising a lot of money this year, by **the looks of** it.*

---

1. immediately
2. in an awkward position where one is forced to make a difficult decision right away
*1. She didn't expect to get an answer for several weeks, but they accepted her application **on the spot**.*
*2. He put me **on the spot** by asking me about my results in front of the group.*

with one voice

warts and all

as a matter of fact

on behalf of

as a rule

unanimously; in unison
*The company's employees approved the policy **with one voice**.*

---

including a person's faults as well as his or her positive qualities
*Parents love their children unconditionally, **warts and all**.*

---

actually; in fact
*From the outside, it seemed like the company was thriving, but **as a matter of fact**, it was on the verge of collapse.*

---

1. in the interest of; in support of
2. as a representative of; in the name of
1. *We are raising money **on behalf of** the local food bank.*
2. *The lawyer wrote a letter **on behalf of** her client, requesting a meeting.*

---

usually; in general
As a rule, we don't hire people without a college degree; however, we might make an exception for him.

one by one

---

on the loose

---

under the weather

In the affirmative

In the negative

individually; in succession; one at a time
When your work seems overwhelming, it can be helpful to deal with your tasks **one by one,** *instead of trying to accomplish everything at once.*

---

out in public
The community was concerned when they heard that a convict had escaped from prison and was **on the loose.**

---

sick; not feeling well
She's not coming in to work today, because she's feeling a bit **under the weather.**

---

positive answer; yes
When he asked the committee if they thought funding the project was a good idea, they responded **in the affirmative.**

---

negative answer; no
She asked the staff if they agreed, but they answered **in the negative.**

EXERCISES

VOCABULARY LIST 1

1. He was able to _____ the outcome without knowing many details.

   a. predict
   b. volunteer
   c. immigrate
   d. violate

2. Because she was a minor, someone had to _____ her on the flight.

   a. relax
   b. volunteer
   c. accompany
   d. restrict

3. When she saw his salary, she _____ in surprise.

   a. approved
   b. restricted
   c. accompanied
   d. exclaimed

4. When he tried to enter the fourth floor, his access card was _____ so he couldn't get in.

   a. denied
   b. approved
   c. accepted
   d. violated

5. Now that the building was _____, she wanted to purchase it as office space.

   a. violated
   b. vacant
   c. denied
   d. exclaimed

VOCABULARY LIST 2

1. The reporter wanted to _____ all of the illegal activity that was going on at the plant.

   a. absorb
   b. expose
   c. unite
   d. purchase

2. The company started to _____ more office space as its profits grew.

   a. purchase
   b. expose
   c. interpret
   d. attract

3. Because he arrived early, he was able to _____ a seat at the front.

   a. revise
   b. influence
   c. interpret
   d. select

4. She wanted to learn the full _____ of the group before she joined.

   a. purchase
   b. select
   c. doctrine
   d. demonstration

5. He found that the best way to teach something new was to _____ how it should be done.

   a. adjust
   b. purchase
   c. demonstrate
   d. select

VOCABULARY LIST 3

1. She wanted to find out who her _____ was so she could ask that person questions.

   a. predecessor
   b. motivation
   c. implementation
   d. corporation

2. He was very good at _____ others to accomplish their goals.

   a. revealing
   b. motivating
   c. implementing
   d. rejecting

3. The email had a very _____ tone to it and lacked a personal touch.

   a. revealing
   b. responding
   c. motivating
   d. corporate

4. He waited for her to _____ before sending another text message.

   a. respond
   b. accelerate
   c. thrive
   d. implement

5. Out of the two of them, she was always the first to _____ a plan.

   a. enhance
   b. strive
   c. formulate
   d. thrive

VOCABULARY LIST 4

1. His teacher _____ a lot of time into tutoring him.

   a. described
   b. modified
   c. investigated
   d. invested

2. It is important to choose the right _____ to ask your supervisor for a letter of recommendation.

   a. factory
   b. investigation
   c. occasion
   d. involvement

3. Everyone in the office liked her _____ demeanor because she was so easy to get along with.

   a. amiable
   b. fluent
   c. invested
   d. involved

4. When the reporter questioned him, he _____ to comment.

   a. invested
   b. declined
   c. modified
   d. anticipated

5. Clothing used to be handmade, but now most of it is produced in _____.

   a. an occasion
   b. an investment
   c. a modification
   d. a factory

VOCABULARY LIST 5

Pair the word on the left with its closest match on the right.

Word	Definition
1. participate	A. be involved
2. versatile	B. swap
3. substitute	C. derive
4. deduce	D. stop
5. prevent	E. adaptable

VOCABULARY LIST 6

Pair the word on the left with its closest match on the right.

Word	Definition
1. convene	A. involve
2. cancel	B. endorse
3. engage	C. congregate
4. confide	D. stop
5. recommend	E. entrust

VOCABULARY LIST 7

Pair the word on the left with its closest match on the right.

Word	Definition
1. approach	A. let in
2. admit	B. come toward
3. feasible	C. check
4. consult	D. possible
5. unify	E. bring together

VOCABULARY LIST 8

1. She completed her portion of the report and planned to _____ his writings after he sent them to her.

   a. insert
   b. cooperate
   c. dominate
   d. facilitate

2. She didn't realize the severe _____ that her actions would have.

   a. cooperation
   b. manipulation
   c. dignity
   d. effect

3. He held his head up high with _____.

   a. manipulation
   b. effectiveness
   c. cooperation
   d. dignity

4. He was always _____ her on her style.

   a. manipulating
   b. facilitating
   c. complimenting
   d. corresponding

5. Rick is helpful to new employees and has a _____ for being a team player.

   a. address
   b. consideration
   c. reputation
   d. protection

VOCABULARY LIST 9

Pair the word on the left with its closest match on the right.

Word	Definition
1. expand	A. focus
2. clarify	B. label
3. concentrate	C. simplify
4. veracity	D. increase
5. categorize	E. correctness

VOCABULARY LIST 10

Pair the word on the left with its closest match on the right.

Word	Definition
1. incorporate	A. diverge
2. position	B. assimilate
3. deviate	C. validate
4. succeed	D. spot
5. justify	E. prosper

VOCABULARY LIST 11

Pair the word on the left with its closest match on the right.

Word	Definition
1. indicate	A. specify
2. develop	B. convention
3. conference	C. evolve
4. estimate	D. revise
5. edit	E. approximate

VOCABULARY LIST 12

1. Because the roads in her city were rough, she needed a _____ vehicle.

   a. durable
   b. display
   c. promoted
   d. consumed

2. He wanted to _____ all possible issues before they occurred.

   a. injure
   b. eliminate
   c. promote
   d. distribute

3. She watched his _____ closely to see if he was bothered by her words.

   a. comparison
   b. depletion
   c. combination
   d. reaction

4. Scientists are now making crops that are not _____ and are unable to produce more crops in the future.

   a. combined
   b. comparable
   c. fertile
   d. conditional

5. After Stephanie underwent surgery, Tim inquired about her _____.

   a. distribution
   b. condition
   c. comparability
   d. elimination

1. The president asked us to shift our _____ to her new project.

   a. focus
   b. tolerance
   c. identification
   d. persuasion

2. Scientists are still trying to understand how some ancient _____ functioned.

   a. identities
   b. societies
   c. guarantees
   d. replacements

3. Because he was doing what most men would do, his actions _____ the male stereotype.

   a. organized
   b. generated
   c. guaranteed
   d. perpetuated

4. She hoped that her stellar job performance would earn her a position in _____.

   a. network
   b. management
   c. society
   d. store

5. He _____ all of the important information for the test in his brain.

   a. stored
   b. replaced
   c. networked
   d. contradicted

1. She definitely wanted to attend the _____, so she bought her tickets months in advance.

   a. validation
   b. convention
   c. equivalent
   d. present

2. They were told to leave everything _____ in the safe.

   a. valid
   b. equivalent
   c. valuable
   d. subtle

3. When he edited the presentation, the most important aspect to him was _____, so that everything looked the same.

   a. consistency
   b. vagueness
   c. conduct
   d. awareness

4. When she joined the club, someone was assigned to _____ her to teach her the basics.

   a. preliminary
   b. present
   c. base
   d. mentor

5. Her new invention greatly _____ the entire process.

   a. mentored
   b. presented
   c. streamlined
   d. based

VOCABULARY LIST 15

Pair the word on the left with its closest match on the right.

Word	Definition
1. universal	A. optimistic
2. domestic	B. widespread
3. associate	C. connect
4. compensate	D. counterbalance
5. positive	E. national

VOCABULARY LIST 16

Pair the word on the left with its closest match on the right.

Word	Definition
1. retire	A. amazing
2. remarkable	B. useful
3. beneficial	C. accessible
4. available	D. leave
5. asset	E. something of value

VOCABULARY LIST 17

Pair the word on the left with its closest match on the right.

Word	Definition
1. potential	A. possibility
2. profit	B. net income
3. phenomenon	C. examine
4. inspect	D. intricate
5. complex	E. spectacle

VOCABULARY LIST 18

1. She had taken the entry level class, so she was already _____ with most of the basic concepts.

   a. familiar
   b. compatible
   c. sufficient
   d. coherent

2. The rules were so _____ that no one knew whether or not they were allowed to ask for outside help.

   a. profound
   b. ambiguous
   c. minuscule
   d. intense

3. Before he could return his defective product, he checked the _____ he had signed when he purchased it.

   a. familiarity
   b. recruit
   c. intensity
   d. contract

4. The job posting was designed to _____ highly-skilled employees.

   a. conceive
   b. medicate
   c. recruit
   d. intensify

5. Although the hotel was not amazing, it was _____ for their work conference.

   a. adequate
   b. conceivable
   c. medical
   d. automatic

1. She performed _____ review of the material before the test to make sure she was prepared.

   a. an objective
   b. a comprehensive
   c. a minimum
   d. a temporary

2. He spent _____ amount of time preparing for the presentation.

   a. an inevitable
   b. a contrary
   c. an ethnic
   d. a considerable

3. She was ecstatic because her review declared her to be _____.

   a. outstanding
   b. legal
   c. previous
   d. minimum

4. The two business partners _____ a fair deal.

   a. minimized
   b. negotiated
   c. contrived
   d. temporized

5. Whenever he negotiated, he did his best to get _____.

   a. an ethnicity
   b. a consideration
   c. a bargain
   d. an objective

1. Signing a waiver was _____ before attending the tour of the plant.

   a. mandatory
   b. incredible
   c. brief
   d. predominant

2. She could _____ to spend her paycheck on a vacation.

   a. brief
   b. appropriate
   c. afford
   d. predominate

3. Their respect was _____; they both looked up to each other.

   a. random
   b. mutual
   c. global
   d. mediocre

4. The manager ordered more _____ every Friday to replace the items sold that week.

   a. employees
   b. mediocrities
   c. clients
   d. merchandise

5. The environment was very important to him, so he did his best to _____ water any chance he got.

   a. conserve
   b. prepare
   c. appropriate
   d. liable

VOCABULARY LIST 21

1. They conducted interviews for months to find the best _____ for the job.

   a. publication
   b. candidate
   c. phase
   d. commerce

2. After she saw the _____ in her report, she rushed to fix it before the presentation.

   a. error
   b. behavior
   c. prerequisite
   d. method

3. The team was no longer able to _____ refreshments after the game.

   a. method
   b. reveal
   c. phase
   d. supply

4. It is important to be _____ when setting expectations for a project.

   a. revolutionary
   b. realistic
   c. stupid
   d. innovative

5. He was known to _____ items to convince customers to make a purchase.

   a. discount
   b. realize
   c. wise
   d. revolve

VOCABULARY LIST 22

1. He liked to remain calm and consider his reactions carefully so that he never ended up in the middle of _____.

   a. an opportunity
   b. a concept
   c. a controversy
   d. an alternative

2. She studied until she became completely _____ in the subject.

   a. resourceful
   b. instance
   c. proficient
   d. conceptualized

3. He found time for everything he loved to do and was able to _____ out his life.

   a. balance
   b. borrow
   c. resource
   d. proof

4. The new business owner _____ money from the bank.

   a. borrowed
   b. conceptualized
   c. proved
   d. alternated

5. She always needed _____ before she would believe anything.

   a. collaboration
   b. proof
   c. opportunity
   d. diversity

VOCABULARY LIST 23

1. The company's profits far exceeded their initial _____.

   a. strategy
   b. forecast
   c. tradition
   d. generation

2. He always liked to figure out his _____ before starting a game.

   a. strategy
   b. generation
   c. tradition
   d. comment

3. She tried her best to listen to the _____, but the material was so boring she almost fell asleep.

   a. circumstance
   b. generation
   c. function
   d. lecture

4. He made a habit of _____ for what he wanted.

   a. emphasizing
   b. lecturing
   c. lobbying
   d. analyzing

5. She regularly performed _____ of the different species of plants growing in the lab.

   a. an analysis
   b. an emphasis
   c. an era
   d. a tradition

VOCABULARY LIST 24

1. The _____ did not change, no matter who was enforcing it.

   a. boon
   b. overall
   c. policy
   d. unison

2. He was very well prepared; _____, the presentation was flawless.

   a. nevertheless
   b. consequently
   c. chiefly
   d. recently

3. There is no doubt about it, she _____ wants to go on vacation.

   a. furthermore
   b. thereby
   c. initially
   d. definitely

4. The store manager required all _____ to be documented.

   a. initials
   b. consequences
   c. transactions
   d. chiefs

5. You should keep your financial records for seven years in case you are ever _____.

   a. audited
   b. initialed
   c. recent
   d. policy

VOCABULARY LIST 25

Pair the word on the left with its closest match on the right.

Word	Definition
1. expert	A. shared
2. joint	B. facts
3. data	C. viewpoint
4. perspective	D. abundant
5. profuse	E. adept

VOCABULARY LIST 26

Pair the word on the left with its closest match on the right.

Word	Definition
1. appearance	A. look
2. individual	B. separate
3. supervise	C. omission
4. exception	D. look after
5. fund	E. supply

IDIOM LIST 1

1. He found testing the limits fun, so he was always _____.

   a. following suit
   b. pushing the envelope
   c. abiding by the rules
   d. backing something up

2. There is no telling what will happen, we will have to wait to see how it all _____.

   a. pans out
   b. accounts for
   c. gives away
   d. backs up

3. Since she is new to the organization, she is looking for someone who _____.

   a. has second thoughts
   b. accounts for
   c. pans out
   d. knows the ropes

4. In high school, I spent all of my afternoons _____ my siblings.

   a. panning out
   b. looking forward to
   c. looking after
   d. looking into

5. I spend each weekday _____ to the weekend.

   a. testing the waters
   b. looking after
   c. looking into
   d. looking forward to

IDIOM LIST 2

1. I never knew he was lying at first, but I finally _____.

   a. touched base
   b. reined him in
   c. saw the light
   d. looked up to him

2. My sister always trusted him and gave him _____.

   a. his own
   b. the benefit of the doubt
   c. saw the light
   d. the information

3. He normally spoke his mind, but today he was careful to _____.

   a. touch base
   b. see the light
   c. off base
   d. hold his tongue

4. She had a meeting with her supervisor to discuss false allegations and _____.

   a. use up
   b. set the record straight
   c. off base
   d. see the light

5. Whenever he went into a match, he made sure to _____ to see what he was up against.

   a. size up the competition
   b. see the light
   c. look up to
   d. off base

IDIOM LIST 3

1. After he was unemployed for six months, people told him to _____ with his salary expectations.

   a. cross paths
   b. run into
   c. lower the bar
   d. end up

2. I don't want to pursue this contract, but _____.

   a. I've crossed paths
   b. my hands are tied
   c. I run into
   d. I see things

3. When she didn't see him for two weeks, she _____ often.

   a. went through with it
   b. asked after him
   c. ended up
   d. got his act together

4. Even though I am confident that I can handle the large project, I know I _____.

   a. have my work cut out for me
   b. crossed paths
   c. will run into
   d. will end up

5. The police _____ in the investigation so that they didn't miss anything.

   a. crossed paths
   b. ended up
   c. run into
   d. left no stone unturned

IDIOM LIST 4

1. Her visits were never planned, she was always _____ unannounced.

   a. going wrong
   b. erring on the side of caution
   c. on the dot
   d. dropping in

2. Now that he is working and has two children, _____ and we don't see him often.

   a. he is going wrong
   b. he is on the dot
   c. his hands are full
   d. on occasion

3. She didn't want to rush the project, so she made sure to _____.

   a. on occasion
   b. go back to the drawing board
   c. go wrong
   d. take her time

4. Even though they didn't always _____ they enjoyed working together.

   a. go back to the drawing board
   b. go wrong
   c. see eye to eye
   d. on the dot

5. He received three different job offers and was having trouble _____ the list.

   a. erring on the side of caution
   b. narrowing down
   c. going wrong
   d. on the dot

IDIOM LIST 5

1. The task at hand was difficult, but she was not willing to _____.

    a. take someone's place
    b. throw in the towel
    c. stay out of
    d. wear thin

2. The mistake was caused by an error on his part, but his coworkers did not want to _____ so they all took the blame together.

    a. throw him under the bus
    b. stay out of it
    c. wear thin
    d. carry out

3. She never wanted to take sides, so she did her best to _____ every argument.

    a. carry out
    b. stay out of
    c. take someone's place
    d. wear thin

4. He was normally so understanding, but these days _____.

    a. he stayed out
    b. he took someone's place
    c. he carried out
    d. his patience was wearing thin

5. She didn't want anyone at work to notice her, so she _____.

    a. wore thin
    b. took someone's place
    c. kept a low profile
    d. carried out

IDIOM LIST 6

1. Since people were talking during the meeting, she wasn't sure she was _____.

    a. thinking better of it
    b. drawing the line
    c. slapping her wrist
    d. getting the message across

2. I was always so sure, but recently he _____ on my beliefs.

    a. cast doubt
    b. thought better of it
    c. drew the line
    d. slapped a wrist

3. Her children were her priority, so she _____ to spend as much time with them as she could.

    a. kept an eye
    b. made do
    c. made sense
    d. made a point

4. He worked the entire day, refusing to _____.

    a. keep an eye
    b. draw the line
    c. take a break
    d. think better of it

5. She was going to call in sick, but realizing her boss would be upset, she _____.

    a. gave him a slap on the wrist
    b. had a piece of cake
    c. drew the line
    d. thought better of it

IDIOM LIST 7

1. He never gave up; he always _____ his task.

   a. stood out
   b. got the best of
   c. wound up
   d. kept at

2. If we keep driving this way, there is no telling where we'll _____.

   a. keep up
   b. wind up
   c. get the best
   d. jump on the bandwagon

3. She wanted to know who had made the calls; she was determined to _____.

   a. jump on the bandwagon
   b. get rid
   c. get to the bottom of it
   d. get the best

4. Even though the stapler didn't work well, he refused to _____ of it.

   a. get the best
   b. jump on the bandwagon
   c. get to the bottom
   d. get rid

5. Before you go on the trip, you should _____ about your finances.

   a. think twice
   b. get the best
   c. jump on the bandwagon
   d. wind down

IDIOM LIST 8

1. She was a free spirit, but her job _____ travelling the world.

   a. sat around
   b. hit the books
   c. hit the nail on the head
   d. kept her from

2. He asked the courier to _____ while he went to get the check.

   a. split hairs
   b. sit tight
   c. show up
   d. hit the nail on the head

3. Before she made any judgments, she was sure to _____.

   a. take all of the information into account
   b. sit tight
   c. show up
   d. split hairs

4. I warned him that meeting the deadline is crucial, but I know that _____.

   a. will split hairs
   b. he hit the nail on the head
   c. goes without saying
   d. he hit the books

5. She was so tired that she decided to _____ early tonight.

   a. split hairs
   b. hit the hay
   c. hit the nail on the head
   d. lend a hand

IDIOM LIST 9

1. He had made a mistake, so he went to the website and wrote an apology in an effort to _____.

   a. off the record
   b. count on
   c. on the fence
   d. save face

2. She was up next for a promotion as soon as her boss retired, so she was just _____.

   a. keeping track
   b. off the hook
   c. biding her time
   d. fielding questions

3. He was the first to hold the role in the company; thus, he _____ others in the future.

   a. counted as
   b. paved the way for
   c. counted on
   d. saved his breath for

4. After she worked 15 days straight, her boss told her to _____ for a while.

   a. take it easy
   b. off the hook
   c. count on
   d. off the record

5. He is always so reliable that I know I can _____ to come through.

   a. off the record
   b. off the hook
   c. pin down the details
   d. count on him

IDIOM LIST 10

1. They expected him to complete the project on target, but he _____ their expectations.

   a. fell short of
   b. let on
   c. put off
   d. passed up

2. Everything in her life was going perfectly and _____.

   a. putting off
   b. falling into place
   c. letting on
   d. passing up

3. The project was _____ nicely.

   a. letting on
   b. icing on the cake
   c. coming along
   d. falling short

4. I don't have time for a long explanation; please _____.

   a. pass up
   b. let on
   c. cut off
   d. cut to the chase

5. He _____ before I could finish my sentence.

   a. cut to the chase
   b. cut me off
   c. let on
   d. took its toll

IDIOM LIST 11

1. She thought that the fire had started in the lobby, but the firefighters _____ that possibility.

   a. gut feeling
   b. ruled out
   c. played it safe
   d. played with fire

2. She was never careless; she always _____.

   a. played with fire
   b. played it safe
   c. turned a blind eye
   d. put down roots

3. I asked him to _____ for the new position.

   a. keep me in mind
   b. turn a blind eye
   c. bring me up to date
   d. put down roots

4. He wanted to _____ his father's company one day.

   a. rule out
   b. cry wolf
   c. take over
   d. put down roots

5. Don't _____; just tell me exactly what happened.

   a. bring me up to date
   b. put down roots
   c. beat around the bush
   d. cry wolf

IDIOM LIST 12

1. She did not want to _____ in their activities.

   a. tie the knot
   b. put the ball in his court
   c. take part
   d. above board

2. You committed the offense; now you have_____.

   a. above board
   b. to tie the knot
   c. third time's a charm
   d. to pay the price

3. I am impartial; I am not one _____ in an argument.

   a. to put the cart before the horse
   b. to be on even keel
   c. above board
   d. to take sides

4. He held three different jobs at the same time and was always _____.

   a. wearing different hats
   b. third time's a charm
   c. tying the knot
   d. above board

5. She always had a way of catching me _____ when I least expected it.

   a. third times a charm
   b. off guard
   c. even keel
   d. above board

1. He was quick to _____, so that he did not waste any time.

    a. run of the mill
    b. get to the point
    c. white collar
    d. blue collar

2. I usually have so much to say, but when I won the award I was _____.

    a. at a loss for words
    b. best of both worlds
    c. full-fledged
    d. run of the mill

3. She always tried to help anyone who was feeling _____.

    a. to the point
    b. on the tip of their tongue
    c. down and out
    d. beside the point

4. We entered into an agreement that was unusually beneficial and, ultimately, it was a _____ situation for both parties.

    a. beside the point
    b. run of the mill
    c. no-win
    d. win-win

5. After her promotion, she was _____ her previous coworkers.

    a. in charge of
    b. best of both worlds
    c. full-fledged
    d. white collar to

1. Her supervisor let her know that she was _____ and should keep heading in the direction she was headed.

    a. in touch
    b. on the fence
    c. on the wrong track
    d. on the right track

2. He was so _____ in his work that he lost track of time.

    a. in the wings
    b. wrapped up
    c. on the fence
    d. in touch

3. When he failed out of school, his parents thought he was _____ and would never find a job.

    a. on the same page
    b. on the fence
    c. on the right track
    d. on the wrong track

4. I am glad that my project manager and I are always _____ because it makes it really easy to work with her.

    a. at a premium
    b. in the wings
    c. on the same page
    d. in the pipeline

5. When she moved away, he made sure to stay _____ with her.

    a. in touch
    b. in wings
    c. in the pipeline
    d. in line

IDIOM LIST 15

1. Even though he was normally a man _____, tonight he had a lot to say.

   a. at the mercy
   b. of few words
   c. fine tuning
   d. on top of

2. I wanted to take on the new project, but the supervisor told me it was _____.

   a. out of the question
   b. on top of
   c. letting the cat out of the bag
   d. fine tuning

3. Our company is _____ of the competition.

   a. once in a blue moon
   b. cutting the corners
   c. light years ahead
   d. easy as pie

4. They tried not to let the argument get _____ because they did not want to draw attention to themselves.

   a. at the mercy of
   b. cutting corners
   c. once in a blue moon
   d. out of hand

5. I was surprised to get an email from him, since I heard from him only _____.

   a. on top of
   b. once in a blue moon
   c. easy as pie
   d. cutting corners

IDIOM LIST 16

1. The su6pply closet was full of _____ and didn't seem to have a complete set of anything.

   a. second wind
   b. mixed emotions
   c. powers that be
   d. odds and ends

2. The sales contest didn't have _____, because Jim had a larger territory.

   a. a last minute
   b. a level playing field
   c. powers that be
   d. mixed emotions

3. She normally kept her opinions to herself, but his outburst was _____, and she finally said something to him.

   a. last minute
   b. second wind
   c. the last straw
   d. mixed emotions

4. He didn't think it was harmful to tell _____, but she didn't appreciate any kind of falsehood.

   a. the light at the end of the tunnel
   b. white lies
   c. last minute
   d. red tape

5. She got along with most new people right away because she was great at _____.

   a. second wind
   b. last minute
   c. mixed emotions
   d. small talk

IDIOM LIST 17

1. Hurry! There is _____.
   a. an upper hand
   b. a clean slate
   c. no time to lose
   d. face value

2. You need to figure out the _____ before you begin the project.
   a. cutting edge
   b. bitter pill
   c. face value
   d. game plan

3. The company was always far advanced above the competition and on the _____.
   a. double-edged sword
   b. zero tolerance
   c. clean slate
   d. cutting edge

4. She was tired during the day so she drank coffee, but she couldn't fall asleep at night because she drank coffee. It was a _____.
   a. vicious cycle
   b. clean slate
   c. face value
   d. zero tolerance

5. He never cared about anyone's past; he always liked to start out friendships with _____.
   a. an Achilles' heel
   b. a clean slate
   c. zero tolerance
   d. a double-edged sword

IDIOM LIST 18

1. Even though we got into a disagreement, there were no _____ afterwards.
   a. ivory towers
   b. hard feelings
   c. recipes for disaster
   d. big pictures

2. When someone is in a rough situation, you will often see their _____.
   a. true colors
   b. ivory tower
   c. bells and whistles
   d. salad days

3. After their disagreement, he apologized and offered an _____.
   a. olive branch
   b. ill-gotten gain
   c. ivory tower
   d. across the board

4. They won the lawsuit but lost their good reputation, so it was a _____.
   a. bell and whistle
   b. big picture
   c. recipe for disaster
   d. hollow victory

5. The new facility was _____.
   a. salad days
   b. big picture
   c. state of the art
   d. at odds

IDIOM LIST 19

1. I don't see her frequently, only every _____.

   a. at stake
   b. on and off
   c. now and then
   d. be that as it may

2. I hadn't heard from him in years and he suddenly called _____.

   a. ahead of time
   b. to speak of
   c. out of the blue
   d. under the table

3. Her policies went _____ with her world views.

   a. hand in hand
   b. on and off
   c. be that as it may
   d. at stake

4. The future is unclear; you never know what will happen _____.

   a. down the road
   b. on her behalf
   c. at stake
   d. to speak of

5. His secretary answered all emails _____.

   a. to speak of
   b. on his behalf
   c. at stake
   d. be that as it may

IDIOM LIST 20

1. You never know what will happen _____, so you need to do your best at all times.

   a. by the book
   b. by all means
   c. over someone's head
   d. down the line

2. She was never one to _____; she said everything to your face.

   a. by all means
   b. back to square one
   c. talk behind someone's back
   d. over someone's head

3. He was absolutely convinced he was right _____.

   a. by no means
   b. beyond the shadow of a doubt
   c. over his head
   d. in view of

4. _____ she is innocent, I don't care what the reporters say.

   a. As far as I am concerned
   b. Back to square one
   c. In view of
   d. By virtue of

5. I thought it would take a while for the copy machine to be completed, but they were done _____.

   a. by the book
   b. for the time being
   c. as usual
   d. in no time

1. _____, I did get a
   haircut; thank you for noticing.

   a. As a matter of fact
   b. In light of
   c. As a rule
   d. On the spot

2. Even though she was
   completely out of shape, she
   won the race _____.

   a. in light of
   b. with one voice
   c. against all odds
   d. by hand

3. _____ the entire city,
   I would like to award you this
   medal of recognition.

   a. With one voice
   b. As yet
   c. In light of
   d. On behalf of

4. He didn't go to work today
   because he was feeling

   _____.

   a. under the weather
   b. by hand
   c. as a rule
   d. on the spot

5. The tiger escaped from the zoo
   and now it is _____ in
   the city.

   a. by hand
   b. on the loose
   c. on the spot
   d. with one voice

ANSWERS

VOCABULARY LIST 1
1. A
2. C
3. D
4. A
5. B

VOCABULARY LIST 2
1. B
2. A
3. D
4. C
5. C

VOCABULARY LIST 3
1. A
2. B
3. D
4. A
5. C

VOCABULARY LIST 4
1. D
2. C
3. A
4. B
5. D

VOCABULARY LIST 5
1. A
2. E
3. B
4. C
5. D

VOCABULARY LIST 6
1. C
2. D
3. A
4. E
5. B

VOCABULARY LIST 7
1. B
2. A
3. D
4. C
5. E

VOCABULARY LIST 8
1. A
2. D
3. D
4. C
5. C

VOCABULARY LIST 9
1. D
2. C
3. A
4. E
5. B

VOCABULARY LIST 10
1. B
2. D
3. A
4. E
5. C

VOCABULARY LIST 11
1. A
2. C
3. B
4. E
5. D

VOCABULARY LIST 12
1. A
2. B
3. D
4. C
5. B

VOCABULARY LIST 13

1. A
2. B
3. D
4. B
5. A

VOCABULARY LIST 14

1. B
2. C
3. A
4. D
5. C

VOCABULARY LIST 15

1. B
2. E
3. C
4. D
5. A

VOCABULARY LIST 16

1. D
2. A
3. B
4. C
5. E

VOCABULARY LIST 17

1. A
2. B
3. E
4. C
5. D

VOCABULARY LIST 18

1. A
2. B
3. D
4. C
5. A

VOCABULARY LIST 19

1. B
2. D
3. A
4. B
5. C

VOCABULARY LIST 20

1. A
2. C
3. B
4. D
5. A

VOCABULARY LIST 21

1. B
2. A
3. D
4. B
5. A

VOCABULARY LIST 22

1. C
2. C
3. A
4. A
5. B

VOCABULARY LIST 23

1. B
2. A
3. D
4. C
5. A

VOCABULARY LIST 24

1. C
2. B
3. D
4. C
5. A

VOCABULARY LIST 25

1. E
2. A
3. B
4. C
5. D

VOCABULARY LIST 26

1. A
2. B
3. D
4. C
5. E

IDIOM LIST 1

1. B
2. A
3. D
4. C
5. D

IDIOM LIST 2

1. C
2. B
3. D
4. B
5. A

IDIOM LIST 3

1. C
2. B
3. B
4. A
5. D

IDIOM LIST 4

1. D
2. C
3. D
4. C
5. B

IDIOM LIST 5

1. B
2. A
3. B
4. D
5. C

IDIOM LIST 6

1. D
2. A
3. D
4. C
5. D

IDIOM LIST 7

1. D
2. B
3. C
4. D
5. A

IDIOM LIST 8

1. D
2. B
3. A
4. C
5. B

IDIOM LIST 9

1. D
2. C
3. B
4. A
5. D

IDIOM LIST 10

1. A
2. B
3. C
4. D
5. B

IDIOM LIST 11

1. B
2. B
3. A
4. C
5. C

IDIOM LIST 12

1. C
2. D
3. D
4. A
5. B

IDIOM LIST 13

1. B
2. A
3. C
4. D
5. A

IDIOM LIST 14

1. D
2. B
3. D
4. C
5. A

IDIOM LIST 15

1. B
2. A
3. C
4. D
5. B

IDIOM LIST 16

1. D
2. B
3. C
4. B
5. D

IDIOM LIST 17

1. C
2. D
3. D
4. A
5. B

IDIOM LIST 18

1. B
2. A
3. A
4. D
5. C

IDIOM LIST 19

1. C
2. C
3. A
4. A
5. B

IDIOM LIST 20

1. D
2. C
3. B
4. A
5. D

IDIOM LIST 21

1. A
2. C
3. D
4. A
5. B